TIME FOR KIDS

BIG BOOK OF WHY

CRAZY, COOL, & OUTRAGEOUS

by Mark Shulman and James Buckley Jr.

Publisher Jim Childs
Vice President, Brand & Digital Strategy Steven Sandonato
Executive Director, Marketing Services Carol Pittard
Executive Director, Retail & Special Sales Tom Mifsud
Executive Publishing Director Joy Butts
Director, Bookazine Development & Marketing Laura Adam
Finance Director Glenn Buonocore
Associate Publishing Director Megan Pearlman
Associate General Counsel Helen Wan
Assistant Director, Special Sales Ilene Schreider
Senior Book Production Manager Susan Chodakiewicz
Design & Prepress Manager Anne-Michelle Gallero
Brand Manager Jonathan White
Associate Prepress Manager Alex Voznesenskiy
Associate Production Manager Kimberly Marshall
Assistant Brand Manager Stephanie Braga

TIME FOR KIDS
Publisher Bob Der
Managing Editor Nellie Gonzalez Cutler
Creative Director Jennifer Kraemer-Smith
Senior Editor Andrea Delbanco

Editorial Director Steven Koepp

Created at Oomf, Inc.
www.Oomf.com
By Mark Shulman and James Buckley Jr.
Designed by Bill Madrid
Educational Consultant: Kara Pranikoff
Researcher/Copy Editor: Beth Adelman
Production: Sandy Gordon
Indexer: Nanette Cardon

Special thanks: Katherine Barnet, Jeremy Biloon, Rose Cirrincione, Erica Davis, Jacqueline Fitzgerald, Christine Font, Jenna Goldberg, Hillary Hirsch, David Kahn, Patty Kelley, Amy Mangus, Amy Migliaccio, Nina Mistry, Dave Rozzelle, Ricardo Santiago, Adriana Tierno, Vanessa Wu

For information on TIME FOR KIDS magazine for the
classroom or home, go to TFKCLASSROOM.com
or call 1-800-777-8600.
For subscriptions to SPORTS ILLUSTRATED KIDS, go to
SIKIDS.COM or call 1-800-889-6007.
Published by TIME FOR KIDS Books,
An imprint of Time Home Entertainment Inc.
135 West 50th Street
New York, NY 10020

ISBN 10: 1-61893-077-X
ISBN 13: 978-1-61893-077-4
Library of Congress Control Number: 2013938712

TIME FOR KIDS is a trademark of Time Inc.

We welcome your comments and suggestions about TIME FOR KIDS Books. Please write to us at:
TIME FOR KIDS Books, Attention: Book Editors, P.O. Box 11016, Des Moines, IA 50336-1016
If you would like to order any of our hardcover Collector's Edition books, please call us at1-800-327-6388 (Monday through Friday, 7 a.m. to 8 p.m., or Saturday, 7 a.m. to 6 p.m., Central Time).

CONTENTS

Welcome to the *Big Book of Why:* *Crazy, Cool, & Outrageous!* This book is overstuffed with more than 1,000 fascinating facts of every kind . . . plus hundreds of eye-catching pictures. It's yet another sizzling-smart book from TIME FOR KIDS!

Here's where you'll find a lot of the questions kids like to ask. And next to those questions are other questions you didn't even *realize* you wanted an answer to! Between these two bright red covers, the *Big Book of Why* gives you the inside story on the natural world, the human world, and other worlds, too.

You're going to have so much fun, you'll want to devour every page. But don't—other smart

HUMAN BODY

Why do **I smile?** Page 17

Why do my ears feel strange when I'm up high?

When you are at high altitude, the air pressure is lower than it is at sea level. The reduced pressure makes your eardrums bulge outward, which can be uncomfortable. What can you do? Swallow or chew gum to let air into a tube between your throat and ears. As the air goes in, it balances the pressure. Pop go your ears, providing sweet relief.

Why are some people able to write with both hands?

For most people, the brain's left or right side is dominant. The left side of the brain controls movement on the right side of the body, and the right side of the brain controls the left side of the body. As a result, people whose brain is dominated by the left side write with their right hands, and vice versa. People with equally strong left and right brains are called ambidextrous. Those people—about 1 in 100—can do things like write, use scissors, and throw balls with both hands.

Why do **teens get zits?**

The bodies of young people, especially teenagers, are constantly going through many changes. During adolescence, the body makes more of an oily substance called sebum. The sebum can sometimes clog pores, which are tiny openings in the skin. Blocked pores cause backups, which create unwanted zits.

COOL!

Some people believe you can discover a person's fate by looking at the lines on their palms. They say these lines can tell your past and even predict your future.

Why does **my foot fall asleep?**

Messages between your brain and the rest of your body can't travel through pinched nerves. If you're sitting in a strange way that pinches nerves, the messages stop arriving and the affected muscles take a nap.

Why do I **have two lungs?**

Your body is designed to protect you. Some body parts, such as lungs and kidneys, are doubled up: two organs do the same job. If there's a problem with one, you're lucky to have a backup. But both lungs aren't exactly the same: the lung on the left side of the body is smaller, which leaves room for the heart.

Why is it **healthy to burp?**

Burping expels gas from the stomach through the mouth. It is also your stomach's way of getting rid of unwanted air. Eating and digesting create all sorts of gases, and swallowing food can sometimes also bring in air. A belch helps clear out the extra air and gas.

Why are **bones white?**

Bones are made of calcium, which is a very light-colored mineral. But inside of the body, bones can appear slightly yellow because they are covered by a thin yellow membrane.

CRAZY!

Believe it or not, you have about 60,000 miles (96,560 km) of blood vessels in your body. Together, you and three friends could stretch 240,000 miles (386,240 km). That distance could reach the moon.

Why do people snore?

We have all sorts of soft, squishy parts in our mouths and throats. When we sleep, they relax along with our other muscles. Snoring happens when air flows through the relaxed throat tissue, causing it to vibrate. Know someone who needs to quiet down? Singing builds up throat muscles. A study showed that singing for 20 minutes every day for three months cuts back on the less-musical nighttime noise.

Why does blood look blue through my skin?

The answer is in your eyes. Light is made up of different colors. When light hits your skin, it appears less red and more blue. That's why blood vessels near the surface of your skin look blue. But human blood doesn't change color—it's always red.

How are left-brain and right-brain people different?

The main part of the brain, the cerebrum, can be divided in two halves. Each part has specific functions. In most people, the right half helps with emotions, creativity, music, and recognizing faces, while the left half is better at language, numbers, and logic. Most people have a stronger, or more dominant, side of the brain.

Why does **crossing my eyes make me see double?**

Normally, your eyes point in the same direction. Your brain naturally combines the images from each eye into one understandable image. But when you cross your eyes, each eye points in a slightly different direction. Your brain doesn't combine the two separate images—so you see see double double.

Why do **my ears ring after a loud sound?**

Sound travels in waves, and loud sounds are like tidal waves. They can bend the tiny hairs in your ears that bring sound to the brain. Some loud noises force your ears into in a small state of shock, and they act like they're still hearing echoes of the noise. The buzzy ringing you hear usually goes away, but some super-loud sounds can cause permanent hearing damage.

How does **laser eye surgery work?**

The shape of your eye contributes to how good your vision is. With a popular procedure called LASIK, doctors use a type of laser to shave a tiny bit off of the eye's cornea. With its new shape, the eyes can focus better, often without glasses. LASIK corrects both near- and farsightedness, and patients can usually see very well on the first day after surgery.

Scientists are working on putting "skin" on robots that is so sensitive, it can feel a butterfly walking on it. The so-called skin is a super-thin film lined with sensors.

COOL!

Why is **my tongue covered in thousands of tiny bumps?**

They're called papillae, but you probably know them as taste buds. Those receptors send a message to the brain about what they are sensing. That sense, called taste, brings in the other senses including smell, touch and sound (crunch!) Your taste buds help you enjoy food, but they also protect you from foods that might harm you, like spoiled milk.

Why do
I have nightmares?

Nightmares are just scary dreams. You might get them because your body is relieving stress, you are ill or you experienced something scary when you were awake. Your most memorable dreams usually happen just before you wake up in the morning.

Why does my face get
red when I'm angry?

Blood rushes to your face and turns your skin red or pink when you get angry. Some scientists think this helped early humans show a scary face to an enemy. But mostly, red happens because your blood pressure goes up as you experience such a strong emotion.

Why do I get nervous?

When you are unsure of what might come next, such as on a test, your body produces more adrenaline. This chemical prepares your body to deal with trouble or run away from it. Blame adrenaline for your upset stomach. But don't run — and don't forget to study.

Why do I smile?

Smiling, like most things you do with your face, is all about communication. Smiling is how your face tells the world that you're feeling good. Scientists think people learn to smile early on because others respond to a smile in a nice way. Evidence also shows that making yourself smile can actually help you feel more positive: when the corners of your mouth turn up, your brain releases a chemical called dopamine that makes you feel happy.

COOL!

A big, sometimes irrational, fear of a certain situation or object is called a "phobia." Common phobias include spiders, heights, thunder, the number 13, and clowns!

Why does **my breath stink** in the morning?

Bacteria in your mouth breaks down tiny food particles around your teeth. In a dry mouth, bacteria can grow rapidly—and bacteria stink. Normally, your spit washes most bacteria away. But at night, you make less saliva, so bacteria grows while you sleep. The obvious solution is to brush your teeth and tongue. But chewing gum, mints, or fresh parsley also gets saliva flowing to help clean out your mouth.

OUTRAGEOUS!

A man in Washington State has the longest eyebrow hair in the world: it measures more than 3.5 inches (8.9 cm) long.

Why do **my eyes look red in some photos?**

Red-eye photos are usually taken at night or indoors. In darker places, your pupils open up more so you can see better. When you take a photo with a flash, the bright light is actually reflecting off of your wide-open retina. That's the part of your eye behind the pupil. Your retina is packed with blood vessels, which is why it looks red.

Why is there **lint** in my belly button?

Your clothes lose little fibers all the time. Most of them fall to the ground or slide off of your skin, but a few get caught in your navel, or belly button. Those fibers can combine into a small clump of lint.

Why do **bruises** change color?

A bruise happens when blood vessels break underneath the skin. The blood that is released loses the oxygen that makes it red, so it looks purple or blue. As the body uses up more components of that blood over time, it can change to look green, yellow, or brown.

Why do **my toes get** "cheese" between them?

Some call it cheese, some call it toe jam. It may sound like food, but it's pretty gross. That gunk between your toes is a potent mix of skin cells, skin oils, sock lint, dirt, and fungus. Being stuck inside a sock keeps it moist . . . and smelly.

Why are **some diseases contagious?**

If a disease is caused by a bacteria or virus that can move from one person to another, it is contagious, or infectious. The germs might be spread by direct contact, by inhaling after a nearby sneeze or cough, or by touching something the infected person has touched. People can spread germs before they even feel sick—and for a week after they get sick.

CRAZY!

The longest recorded case of hiccups lasted for 68 years!

Why do **medical staff wear masks?**

Masks protect both the patient and the health care provider. Bacteria and viruses can spread easily from close contact with another person. Doctors, dentists, and nurses wear masks to make sure they don't exchange unwanted germs with their patients.

Why do vaccinations work?

Shots hurt for a few seconds, but they protect you for a long time. Vaccines contain weak (or dead) bits of a harmful germ. Your body's natural illness-fighting ability—the immune system—learns to make customized cells called antibodies that attack that type of germs. When your body faces that germ again in the future, it will have a better chance to fight back.

Why are colds called colds?

Long ago, before people knew about bacteria and viruses, they recognized that most sniffly, sneezy, coughing illnesses happened in the winter. So they called that type of illness a cold. What they didn't know was that low humidity—the moisture in the air— helps germs live in the winter, not low temperatures.

Why do teeth get cavities?

When you eat sugar, it stays on your teeth even after you finish the food. But the eating isn't done: bacteria in your mouth eats away at the sugar. As bacteria eat, they change the sugar to plaque, which in turn eats into your teeth. The places where plaque stays too long become the holes we call cavities.

ANIMALS

Why do **sharks have so many teeth?** Page 28

22

Why do **male lions roar?**

For lions, roaring is like talking. Different sounds can express different things. Male lions roar to claim their territory, as if to say "This place is mine!" Sometimes they roar to call lionesses. Roars can be heard for miles, which is helpful since lions often live in large, flat areas.

Why do **some animals' eyes shine at night?**

Many animals, including dogs, cats, deer and ferrets, have a special layer of tissue at the back of their eye called the tapetum lucidum, which is Latin for "bright cloth." It helps the animal see better at night. When light passes through the retina and hits this surface, it reflects back with a cool color—yellow, green, or even turquoise.

Why do **tigers have stripes?**

Tigers are outstanding hunters, thanks in part to their stripes. Stripes help tigers hide as they sneak up on prey. The stripes serve as camouflage in the tall grasses and forests where they hunt.

Why do **animals migrate?**

To migrate means to move from one place to another and back, year after year. Changes in the seasons affect animals' habitat, so many animals migrate to find food and water where the weather is better. Some animals also migrate to find safer places to raise their young. Migrations occur by land, sea, and sky.

OUTRAGEOUS!

Wombats are small mammals that live in Australia. Their poop is cube-shaped, like a handful of dice.

Why do **gorillas thump their chest?**

Gorillas, like all primates, communicate using sounds and gestures. Male gorillas pound their chest to intimidate other gorillas, showing off their super strength and dangerous size.

Why do people think frogs cause warts?

Many types of frogs have crusty bumps on their skin that look like warts. For centuries, people believed that touching these bumps could spread warts. In truth, warts are caused by a virus.

Why do snakes stick out their tongue so often?

Snake use their tongues, along with their nostrils, to gather information that helps them survive. Their tongue can sense odors in the air. That's how they find food or predators. A small part in the roof of the mouth, called the Jacobson's organ, gathers messages from the tongue and delivers them to the snake's brain.

Why do **tortoises** live so long?

Three factors help tortoises live for more than 100 years. They have a thick, armored shell, so they're hard to kill. They live on islands far from most possible predators, including humans. And they keep a slow pace: By growing slowly and living slowly, they also age slowly.

CRAZY!

A tortoise named Jonathan, who lives on St. Helena island in the Atlantic Ocean, is believed to be the oldest animal alive. He's more than 178 years old!

Why do **chameleons** change color?

Chameleons in Africa use their color-changing powers to communicate with each other. A chameleon looking for love will turn bright, fun colors. A sad or scared chameleon becomes dark or even black. Smaller chameleons called anoles change from green to brown to hide from predators.

Why are so many people afraid of spiders?

We're not born afraid of spiders. It's something we learn. Fear of spiders is so common, it has its own name: arachnophobia. Some scientists think humans are naturally worried about animals that move quickly, as spiders do, and the fact that some spiders are poisonous certainly adds to the fear factor.

Why are stingrays dangerous?

At the end of a stingray's tail is a sharp, poisonous barb or spike. The stingray can use it as a weapon by whipping it into an animal or a person when it feels threatened. If it hits a vital organ, the poisonous barb can kill a large fish or a person within minutes.

Why do sharks have so many teeth?

Sharks need extra teeth because they lose so many of them. Their teeth come out easily when they bite into or chew their prey. Their teeth grow in a series of rows, allowing new ones to move up when the old ones fall out. Some shark species can have thousands of teeth during the course of their lifetime.

Why should **people be very careful around hippos?**

More people in Africa are hurt or killed by the hippo than by another other mammal. The main reason: people and hippos often come together in rivers and streams. The hippos guard their water territory fiercely and will attack humans who they think are threatening.

CRAZY!

One of the most poisonous animals in the world looks like a blob of goo. The box jellyfish doesn't look scary, but it has a sting that can kill large fish ... or even people.

Why can **tiny mosquitoes be deadly?**

When a mosquito infected with a disease called malaria bites someone, the disease can pass into the person's bloodstream. Without treatment, it can be deadly. One million people die each year of malaria; most of them are children in Africa. Mosquitoes can also pass around dengue fever and yellow fever, mostly in tropical parts of the world.

Why do **birds survive sitting on power lines?**

What's keeping birds from being barbecued on high-voltage wires? Birds don't get shocked because they're touching only one wire. They don't create a circuit, which is an electrical path for the power to travel through. It would be bad news for birds if they touched a wire and something touching the ground at the same time.

Why are condors bald?

Condors eat carrion, otherwise known as already-dead animals. They prefer large carrion, like sheep or deer. Condors have to plunge their heads into the carcass of their prey to be able to eat. Their bald heads come out cleaner than they would if they had feathers. It's gross to think about, but the design actually keeps condors quite tidy.

CRAZY!

The bald eagle isn't bald—it has a head full of white feathers. Condors, vultures, baby penguins and the bare-faced bulbul truly have hairless heads. Bald is beautiful!

Why do crows chase hawks?

Have you ever seen a group of crows swooping and diving around a hawk in mid-air? They're not playing . . . they're chasing. Hawks are kind of like cannibals. They try to eat baby birds, including crows. The adult crows are protecting their nests by chasing attackers away.

Why do ostriches put their head to the ground?

It's not what you may think— ostriches don't actually bury their head in the sand to hide. Ostriches are huge, powerful birds. They attack or run very fast—hiding is not in their nature. That bent-over ostrich is most likely a concerned mother, checking the eggs in her shallow nest.

Why are some doves called pigeons?

Cities are full of them. Statues are covered by them. The birds in question aren't officially pigeons. They're rock doves. The rock dove has lived on cliffs and along steep mountains in Europe and Africa for hundreds of thousands of years. When cities were built up, with steep walls and streets full of garbage, the rock dove found a new home and a new name.

Why do **dolphins jump out of the water?**

Jumping lets dolphins search for food far ahead. Dolphins can also communicate with other dolphins by jumping, in addition to grabbing a fresh breath of air. Plus, many scientists think the dolphins might just be having fun.

OUTRAGEOUS!

The largest shark – the whale shark – can measure larger than 40 feet long (12 m). It's intimidating, but not especially dangerous, because they have no teeth. They eat only small fish and plankton.

Why don't **electric eels zap themselves?**

The answer is shocking: They probably do . . . but it doesn't bother them. Eels can put out about 50 times more electricity than a car battery. The eels can't avoid being zapped by it because electricity moves through saltwater very easily, but their body tissue insulates them from much of the shock. The animals have evolved to survive the same zap that stuns smaller fish.

Why are tropical fish so colorful?

Scientists believe bright colors can serve as camouflage for tropical fish, and can help them attract mates. Sometimes poisonous fish use their bright colors to warn away would-be predators. Another theory is that reef fish see more colors than humans can, so they have to be colorful to be recognized.

Why do fish lay so many eggs?

Many fish actually eat fish eggs. To give their babies a better chance of survival, fish produce thousands or even millions of eggs. Also, most male fish fertilize the female's eggs after they have hatched, which is not a very efficient way to reproduce. By producing more eggs, the fish have a greater chance of successful breeding, and the survival of their species.

Why do fish swim in schools?

Sticking together underwater gives fish many advantages. They can swim faster in a group than they can when they go it alone. Also, if one fish finds food, all the others benefit. But perhaps the biggest advantage of schooling is that it makes it harder for a predator to single out one fish for an attack.

Why don't **beavers get splinters?**

When beavers chew wood, their lips slip behind their teeth to prevent slivers in their mouth. Plus, they mostly chew soft or wet wood that doesn't have many splinters. Legend has it that once young beavers get a splinter, they learn never to get one again.

Why shouldn't **dogs eat chocolate?**

The chemical in chocolate that makes it taste so good, theobromine, exits our body quickly. The body of a dog, however, can't get rid of it quickly enough. It can cause trouble with the dog's heart, digestive system, and brain that can even be deadly. Dark chocolate, which contains more theobromine, can be especially dangerous to dogs.

Why don't cats like water?

Most cats can't swim and don't like the way water feels on their fur. Cats would rather lick their fur to clean it than be bathed in any other way. You can teach some cats to tolerate water if you start training them when they're very young.

Why do cows have so much gas?

The stomach of a cow has four compartments, each filled with bacteria that helps digest food. The bacteria produces a gas called methane that cows release from both ends. Since they eat often, they have gas often, too. With more than 1.5 billion cows in the world, there's no gas shortage!

Why do horses let us ride them?

Like many animals, horses live in groups. Animals in any herd learn to cooperate and understand that different animals have different roles within the group. When horses are properly raised by humans, they may learn to accept their role as the animal who carries people and other burdens.

COOL!

One breed of cat, called the Turkish Van, is a good swimmer and seems to enjoy the water. Adults have water-resistant fur.

Why do caterpillars change into butterflies?

Caterpillars can't have babies and they can't fly. In order to mate and lay eggs, they have to move from the early caterpillar stage into the mature butterfly stage. Changing from a bug that walks to one that flies helps them find new places to live.

Why do ants have such a good sense of direction?

Ants have to leave their nests to find food, so they also need to know how to get back home. The first ants marching in a line leave a chemical trail for the others to follow. Ants that come along later combine this trail with things they see to make a mental map. Some scientists think ants count their steps or use the sun to navigate.

CRAZY!!

Some cicadas hibernate for 17 years between mating cycles. After all that time, they come out from underground to mate and lay eggs.

Why do flies like dead things?

Flies will eat just about anything, whether it is alive or dead. But eating something dead is much easier. This is also why many types of flies lay their eggs in dead animals. When the babies hatch, there's very handy food to feed them.

NATURE

Why do
hurricanes form?

Why are **some storm clouds so dark?**

The brightness of clouds depends on their size. Thinner clouds are brighter because they let more sunlight shine through. Thicker clouds, such as thunderstorm clouds, are darker because they don't let as much sunlight through.

Why does it **sometimes smell like rain?**

When rain is on the way, the air pressure drops. This lower pressure makes it easier for all kinds of odors to come out. So while it doesn't smell exactly like rain, it smells like all the things you can't normally smell in nice weather, when the air pressure is higher.

CRAZY!

Smog happens when smoke, pollution, sunlight and fog mix together and hang around, usually in large cities. Smog = Smoke + Fog.

Why do we get hail instead of snow?

Hailstones are frozen raindrops that are a product of a thunderstorm. Sleet and hail form when the air temperature fluctuates within the cloud and between the ground and the cloud. Snow is different: it's water vapor that freezes into ice crystals without ever becoming a liquid.

Why does lightning often strike trees?

When electrical particles are produced by storm clouds, they are attracted to oppositely-charged particles on the ground. The meeting of the two types of charges creates a lightning strike. Trees are connected to the ground but stand tall, often making them the first thing lightning encounters as it strikes down from the sky.

How can people predict weather?

Meteorologists are like a detective studying Earth's atmosphere for clues about weather conditions. They gather evidence, including temperature, wind speed and direction, time of year, and humidity. This evidence (and help from computers and mathematical models) helps predict weather that is on the way.

Why do **hurricanes form?**

Warm ocean water heats the air above it. The warm air rises, and cooler air rushes in beneath to replace it. Some storms remain small, but others gather warm ocean moisture and the rushing winds move faster and faster. Winds spin around the "eye" at the storm's center creating either a tropical storm or a hurricane, depending on the winds' speed. Wind speeds of more than 74 mph (119 kph), are classified as hurricanes.

COOL!

About 1,000 tornadoes strike the United States each year. Most tear through a zone in the Midwest called Tornado Alley, which extends north from Texas to South Dakota. More tornadoes hit this area than almost anywhere else in the world.

Why do **rivers flood?**

Rivers normally flow within their banks, but too much water can cause a river to overflow, like a bathtub when you leave the water running. When there's a lot of rain or melting snow, all that water flows into the river from many directions. The water level rises above the riverbanks, creating a flood.

Why do **most forest fires start?**

Wildfires are a part of the natural cycle of forests. They help clear dead trees and make way for new growth. But people cause 80 to 90 percent of the wildfires in the United States each year, mostly by accident, and lightning causes most of the other wildfires. Lightning fires usually burn more acres than human-caused fires. Why? The human-caused fires are usually in places that are easier for firefighters to reach quickly.

Why do **tsunamis happen?**

A tsunami, which means "harbor wave" in Japanese, is formed in the sea. It is triggered by a disturbance in the ocean floor, most often an earthquake, which forces a massive movement of water. The waves spread in all directions, moving as fast as 500 miles an hour. The waves slow down as a tsunami nears shallow water, but they can still be fast and destructive as they strike the shore.

43

Why do bananas turn black?

Bananas grow in tropical climates, where it's warm nearly all the time. They don't grow well in the cold. When bananas do get cold, as they would in a refrigerator, cells in their peels break down, releasing chemicals that turn their skin black or brown and make their insides mushy.

How do grapes become raisins?

Grapes contain a lot of water inside of their thin skins. When most of the water is removed, what's left is a raisin. Most raisins are made by drying the grapes under the hot summer sun. It takes four pounds of grapes to make just one pound of raisins.

Why are **tomatoes really fruit?**

There are two requirements for being a fruit. Fruits must have seeds and must come from a flowering plant. The tomato technically meets both requirements, as do green beans, peppers, and corn. But even though the tomato is technically a fruit, the U.S. Department of Agriculture lists it as a vegetable.

Why are there **so many kinds of apples?**

Different apples are used in different ways. Over the years, farmers have bred different apples that are better for eating, baking pies, creating applesauce, making juice, and so on. More than 2,500 kinds of apples are grown in the United States, but only about 15 are sold in large numbers.

Why do **some pumpkins get so big?**

Some farmers specialize in growing giant pumpkins. With the right soil, seeds, and careful tending, pumpkins can grow to enormous sizes. The world record pumpkin weighed in at 2,009 pounds (911 kg)—about as much as an American bison. Pumpkin seeds that get big results include Prizewinner Hybrid, Atlantic Giant, Mammoth Gold, and Big Max.

Why are some trees called evergreens?

Trees that do not change color, and do not drop their leaves are called evergreens. Their leaves are thick, sharp, and pointy. Pine trees are a common type of evergreen. Less common are the giant redwood sequoias of the Pacific Northwest.

OUTRAGEOUS!

Flowers are supposed to smell sweet, right? Well, don't get a whiff of the massive Titan arum. This plant, which only flowers every four to six years, smells like rotting meat!

Why do some plants eat bugs?

Most plants get nutrients from soil. Bug-eating plants usually grow in soil that doesn't provide everything they need to live, so they must eat bugs in order to survive. Meat-eating plants like the Venus flytrap and bladderworts have evolved clever ways to trap their prey.

Why are fallen logs usually full of bugs?

What is a tree? For a human, it can create shade. For a bird, it can be a home. For bugs, trees can be a source of food. Fallen trees and logs are easy pickings for the many types of bugs who eat them. Logs also make safe and sturdy homes for bugs and other animals.

Why do roses have thorns?

Sharp, pointy thorns help a rose protect itself. Roses and other flowers taste good to animals, and it's hard for flowers to defend themselves. Thorns and needles are a defensive strategy—they poke the sensitive mouths of animals, scaring away would-be predators.

Why is grass often wet in the morning?

The wetness is called dew. Air almost always holds water vapor. When the temperature is warm, air can hold a lot of water vapor. But when the temperature drops, it can hold less. So when air cools off at night, some of the water vapor turns to liquid and falls to the ground, where it becomes dew.

Why do some places ban plastic bags?

Every year, billions of plastic bags are distributed, and few are recycled. The flimsy bags are harmful to the environment and to wildlife. Animals eat them and die, and the bags take hundreds of years to break down in landfills. Plus, making these bags takes millions of barrels of oil. To help the environment, many Americans have made the switch from paper and plastic bags to reusable grocery bags. In some cities, it's the law.

Why don't we recycle Styrofoam?

Styrofoam is a brand name for a material called polystyrene. The squishy white stuff is made from oil, so it's very expensive to recycle safely. We have many ways to re-use aluminum and plastic, for example, but almost none for polystyrene, so it ends up staying in landfills for a long, long time.

Why do scientists say the planet is getting warmer?

Scientists believe that human beings are partly to blame for the Earth's changing climate. Every year, people burn more and more fuel, such as coal, oil, and gas. The gasses they produce fill the sky, forming a hazy blanket around the earth that traps heat inside its atmosphere. Because that heat stays around for a long time, the Earth has been slowly heating up . . . a process called global warming, or climate change.

Why are **some rainbows double?**

Rainbows form when sunlight is broken up as it passes through raindrops. The rain breaks the white light into all its colors, like a prism. A double rainbow happens when the light also reflects the rainbow itself. It's actually a mirror image— the colors appear in the opposite order: VIBGYOR-ROYGBIV.

COOL!

Sixth-grade students in Santa Barbara, California, formed the "Paper Not Plastic" campaign in 2012. Their website, posters, and community activities helped make a plan to ban plastic grocery bags in their city.

Why do **we celebrate Earth Day?**

In 1969, a terrible oil spill hit the beach in Santa Barbara, California. Shocked by this, a U.S. senator from Wisconsin named Gaylord Nelson helped organize the first Earth Day as a celebration of our planet, and a rallying point to protect it. Enthusiasm for Earth Day helped persuade lawmakers to pass the 1970 Clean Air Act and to create the Environmental Protection Agency. Each April 22, people worldwide gather to show concern for our planet.

49

EARTH

Why is the
Grand Canyon so huge? Page 54

50

Why is it **hotter near the Equator?**

The Equator is an imaginary line drawn around the middle of the planet, exactly between the North and South Poles. As the Earth moves around the sun, the temperatures in the planet's midpoint are higher than at the northern and southern ends of the planet. That's because the Equator receives mostly direct sunlight year-round.

sun rays →

Why is the **Prime Meridian in Greenwich, England?**

Earth is divided into 24 north-to-south lines of longitude, also called meridians. Each meridian is a different time zone. The Prime Meridian is the line of 0 longitude, which is the imaginary line that divides the earth into two halves, or hemispheres. This line passes through the Royal Observatory in Greenwich, England. At a meeting of scientists in 1884, that site was chosen.

axis

North Pole

axis

Arctic Circle

Tropic of Cancer

Equator

Tropic of Capricorn

Why do imaginary lines divide the Earth?

The Tropic of Cancer and the Tropic of Capricorn are imaginary lines that circle the Earth. Between those lines lie the equator and a region called the tropic zone, an area known for having steady high temperatures. The tropic lines got their names 2,000 years ago from stars that could be seen along those lines during the summer and winter solstices.

CRAZY!

The area near the Equator sometimes has very little wind. Early sailors could get stuck in those waters for weeks waiting for wind to pick up in the "doldrums."

Why is the Earth's axis tilted?

The Earth's axis is the imaginary pole that our planet spins around, creating night and day. The axis is tilted 23.5 degrees. Most scientists think we got our tilt during a long-ago collision with another planet. The tilt gives us changing temperatures, making Earth perfect for supporting life . . . so it was a lucky bounce.

Why is the **Grand Canyon so huge?**

A canyon is a deep, narrow valley with steep sides. The Grand Canyon, in Arizona, is more than one mile (1.6 km) deep in places. Its upper rim measures an average of 10 miles (16 km) from edge to edge. The rushing Colorado River carved out this amazing spectacle over millions of years. During that time, the river washed away tremendous amounts of rocks and dirt, leaving behind this cavernous canyon.

Why do **islands stay in the same place?**

Islands are not rafts! Most islands are attached to the sea floor, just like continents. In many cases, islands are the highest parts of mountains that rise up from the bottom of the sea. Some islands are the tops of huge volcanoes, and others are formed from thousands of years of built-up coral.

Why do stalactites form in caves?

Stalactites look like icicles hanging in caves. They appear where water drips from the ground above a cave. The water contains carbon dioxide, calcium, and other minerals. Over many years, the "rocky" water drips through cracks in the cave ceiling and dries out in a cone shape. Each drip makes the cone just a little bit longer.

Why are some mountains snowy even in the summer?

Even when it's warm and sunny at the base of certain mountains, snow can still be seen on top of high peaks. The higher up you go from sea level, the colder it gets. Some mountain peaks are so high that the air never warms up, even on the hottest days down below. Plus, when there's a large amount of snow, it can take a long time to melt, even in sunny weather.

COOL!

Stalagmites are upside-down stalactites, pointing upward. Here's how to remember the names: StalaCtites (with a C) are on the Ceiling. StalaGmites (with a G) are on the Ground.

Why is gold so valuable?

The element called gold is rare, as most of the Earth's gold lies at its core. It is also beautiful, strong, and flexible enough to be made into all kinds of things, both practical and beautiful.

Why is quartz so shiny?

Rocks are usually made up of a mixture of minerals. Quartz, however, is almost always made from pure silicon dioxide. The silicon dioxide makes quartz appear almost clear and shiny. Small amounts of other minerals can change the color of quartz to green, pink, purple, or even brown.

How do we know how old the Earth is?

The answer is in the rocks. Some elements are radioactive. Over a long period of time, those elements change and stop being radioactive. Special machines measure how radioactive a rock's elements are, and a technique called radioactive dating lets scientists calculate how old Earth is—about 4.5 billion years old.

Why is sand different colors?

Sand is made of tiny pieces of larger rocks. If the original rocks were yellow, black, pink, or white, then the sand they make will be the same color. For example, sand on volcanic beaches in Hawaii is black like the lava that makes it. Likewise, the pink coral that is common in Bermuda becomes pink sand.

Why did dinosaur bones turn into fossils?

Many dinosaurs died in places where soft rocks and soil protected their bones from disintegrating. Then, over time, the calcium in their bones was replaced by various minerals, which eventually hardened to form long-lasting fossils.

Why are the North and South Poles so cold?

Neither end of the Earth gets much sunlight, and what they do get is neither direct nor warm. Plus, much of the sunlight is reflected back into space from the ice that covers so much of the polar regions. The icy terrains also do not leave room for much exposed land, which usually helps absorb the heat of the sun.

Why is Antarctica a continent?

Home to the South Pole, Antarctica is covered by ice year-round, up to three miles thick. Under all that ice is a large mass of actual land that is about the size of the continental United States, plus most of Mexico. Its size and land mass give this rocky terrain at the bottom of the world status as a continent. Massive shelves of ice cling to its sides, a necklace of sea ice surrounds it, and colossal icebergs float near its shores.

Why are scientists drilling ice way down below Antarctica?

They're actually studying history. The ice on Antarctica was built up over many centuries. The core samples they drill are like super-long icicles dug from way below the surface. The ice they retrieve is packed with clues about the weather and atmosphere in ancient times.

Why did **explorers race to the North and South Poles?**

By the early 1900s, most of the world had been explored. Though few new adventures remained, the North and South Poles had not yet been reached. Several nations sent teams to try to get there first. In 1909, American explorers Robert Peary (right) and Matthew Henson won the race to the North Pole. Norway's expedition, led by Roald Amundsen, was first to reach the South Pole in 1911.

Why don't **penguins live at the North Pole?**

Penguins can live at the South Pole because way down under the thick ice, there's land. The land means the ice is stable, so they can tend their nests, make shelter, and otherwise survive when they're not in the ocean. Since the North Pole is made of floating ice that is always moving and shifting, it's not the best place to call home.

Why are **oceans blue?**

Beauty—and color—are in the eyes of the beholder. The light we see is made of many colors at once. Ocean water absorbs colors like red and orange, but blue wavelengths are reflected, making the ocean appear to be blue. Other colors in the sea come from plants, dirt, and pollution.

Why can **sea mammals drink seawater?**

Some marine mammals, like whales and seals, can drink seawater and survive. Their extra-efficient kidneys help them remove excess salt through their urine. But the fact that they can drink salt water doesn't mean they do. Most marine mammals likely don't drink much seawater at all. Some sea animals get all the water they need from eating fish, while seals sometimes eat snow to get water.

Why do whirlpools start?

When water spins down the toilet bowl after a flush, it's making a whirlpool motion. Whirlpools happen in the ocean, too. When two currents moving in opposite directions meet, a whirlpool can form, spinning around and around. Some scientists think these whirlpools actually help slow global warming by gathering and drawing in carbon from the air.

OUTRAGEOUS!

A "red tide" happens when algae (tiny plants that live in the ocean) suddenly bloom in huge numbers, turning the ocean red. Red tides remove oxygen from the water, and can be deadly for fish.

SPACE

Why can **rockets reach space?**
Page 72

Why does **the sun appear yellow?**

The sun is a star, and the color of a star depends on how hot it is. When you light a fire, the coolest part at the top is red, the hotter part in the middle is yellow, and the hottest part at the bottom is blue. Stars are the same. Yellow stars, like our sun, are in the middle of the heat range, with a temperature of about 10,000°F (5,500°C). Some places, called sunspots, appear darker because they are cooler than the rest of the sun.

Why won't **the sun shine forever?**

All stars have a nuclear reaction going on inside them. Eventually, millions of years from now, our sun will run out of nuclear fuel to burn and its core will collapse. The outer gaseous layers of the sun will expand into space, leaving behind a bare core about the size of Earth. Over the next several billion years, this bare core will burn out and cool off. That will be the end of the sun. But relax, you'll miss it!

Why do **people bounce around on the moon?**

How high could you jump on the moon? Gravity on the surface of the moon is only one-sixth as strong as it is on Earth. This means you could jump about six times higher. In other words, if on Earth you can jump up about 10 inches (25 cm), then on the moon you can jump 60 inches. That's five feet (152 cm) straight up!

COOL!

Sometimes the sun shoots out massive amounts of magnetic energy, called solar flares. They can influence the weather on Earth, disturb radio communications, damage satellites, and even cause temporary electrical blackouts.

Why doesn't the moon crash into Earth?

The gravity of the Earth is stronger than the gravity of the moon, so the moon should get pulled into the Earth . . . right? Wrong. The Earth and the moon are both moving. The direction of their movement would actually take them right past each other. Gravity manages to balance this dance just enough to keep both bodies from flying out of their intended orbits or colliding.

Why can't **people live on Mars?**

Humans could not breath on Mars because of its very thin atmosphere. Plus, it's really cold there—on average, the temperature on Mars is about 80°F below zero (60° C below zero). Still thinking of moving there? Huge storms of red dust swirl across Mars, sometimes covering the entire planet. These giant storms can last for months.

Why do **Jupiter and Saturn have so many moons?**

The larger the planet, the greater the gravity. The tremendous gravity on Jupiter and Saturn, our biggest planets, makes them more likely to trap the dust, debris, and rocks that float around our solar system. When a really big rock gets caught in a planet's gravity, that's called a moon. Both planets have more than 50 moons, and new moons are still being discovered every year.

Why does Jupiter have a giant spot on its surface?

Jupiter's Great Red Spot is a giant spinning storm that has been around since at least the 1600s. The storm system is large enough to engulf Mars and Earth together. Storms on our largest planet get so big and last so long because Jupiter has gas layers and liquid layers, but no solid land. Without land masses, there's little to stop the energy of a storm.

CRAZY!

One of Jupiter's largest moons, Io, has more than 400 active volcanoes.

Neptune

Pluto

Why do Neptune and Pluto switch places?

Neptune is the second to last planet in our solar system and Pluto is the last, right? Usually, but not always. It takes the dwarf planet Pluto about 248 Earth years to circle the sun. For 20 of those years, Pluto's irregular orbit brings it closer to the sun than Neptune. The last time that happened was from 1979 to 1999; before that was in the 1700s. If you missed it last time, chances are you won't see it again.

Why are **supernovas so huge?**

When a giant star starts running out of nuclear fuel, it shrinks and grows hotter and denser. Eventually, all of the nuclear reactions inside of it stop. In less than a second, the temperature rises to more than 100 billion degrees as the atoms in the star's core are crushed together. There's a lot of energy stored in so much heat. It's all released in a violent explosion, and the exploding star is called a supernova. Supernovas, which can release more light in a few days than 100 million suns, can be seen from very far away.

Why do **stars form?**

A star develops from a giant, slowly spinning cloud of gas and dust. The cloud is mostly made up of the chemical elements hydrogen and helium, but it also contains atoms of other elements and microscopic particles of dust. As this cloud spins, the stuff inside it gets pushed into clumps that are packed tighter and tighter until a nuclear reaction starts. A star is born!

COOL!

Our sun stands alone, but about three-quarters of all stars are part of a binary system—a pair of stars that formed so close together that they orbit each other.

What is **the Big Bang Theory?**

According to a well-tested theory, our universe formed in an instant. Scientists believe the Big Bang—a giant burst of energy—created the universe about 13.8 billion years ago. Before the Big Bang, everything that now exists in the universe was crammed together into a hot, dense point called a singularity. As this singularity started to cool it expanded rapidly, and our universe was formed.

Why do **stars twinkle?**

What we see as twinkling is really caused by movements in Earth's atmosphere. Starlight enters the atmosphere as straight rays of light. Twinkling occurs because air movements constantly change and wiggle the path of the light as it comes through the air.

Why do **comets have names?**

Comets are named for the people who discover them. Halley's Comet, for example, was named for English astronomer Edmond Halley. Space probes have also spotted many comets—the European Space Agency's Solar and Heliospheric Observatory is the greatest single comet finder of all time. It spotted 2,000 comets in just five years.

Why is **there only one Solar System?**

The universe is infinite, yet there is only one solar system. How is that possible? It's all in the name. There are countless groups of planets orbiting a star, called star systems. But if the star is called Sol, the name of our sun, that star system is called the Solar System. There's only one Sol.

Why do **we see comets?**

Comets orbit the sun in a regular path, but most orbits take them deep into space before they come back toward the sun. Occasionally, a comet's orbit takes it through the inner part of the solar system, where we can see it. Some comets take about 200 years to orbit the sun once, and some take even longer. The famous Halley's Comet is visible from Earth for only a short period about every 76 years. It will next be visible in 2061.

Why do some stars become shooting stars?

Shooting stars are actually meteoroids—bits of dust and rock that blow off of comets, asteroids, and even the moon and Mars. Most meteorites burn up when they enter the Earth's atmosphere. Those that don't burn up become falling stars. They fall very fast, which makes them super-hot as they enter Earth's atmosphere. As they burn, they glow.

Why do comets have long tails?

A comet is a solid mass of frozen gas, ice, and dust, like a big dirty snowball. Comets move in an elliptical orbit around the sun. Heat from the sun melts the outside layer of the snowball into water vapor. Then radiation from the sun, known as solar wind, blows the vapor out into a long tail of dust and gasses that can be many miles long.

CRAZY!

Meteors that make it down to Earth and hit the ground are called meteorites. Most are the size of a grain of sand, but some are large enough to do damage. In 1908, an explosion known as the Tunguska Event destroyed 770 square miles of forest in Siberia, Russia. It is believed to have been caused by a giant meteorite.

Why are there still footprints on Earth's moon?

All the astronauts, rovers, and spacecraft that have visited the moon leave a permanent mark. The moon doesn't have any air or atmosphere, so there's no wind or rain to wipe them away. All previous prints are presumably still visible in the lunar dust.

Why can rockets reach space?

The gravity of the Earth is very strong and pulls everything toward its surface. It takes a lot of energy to overcome that pull. Rockets are mostly filled with fuel that burns fast, pushing the rocket beyond our atmosphere. Once they reach space, they need far less fuel to fly.

Why was the space shuttle different than other spacecraft?

The space shuttle was the first spacecraft that was designed to take off and land over and over again. All other vehicles that have carried astronauts into space were designed for one-time use. NASA retired its 30-year-old shuttle program in 2011 because the space vehicles were too old and expensive to operate.

Why do **astronauts exercise in space?**

Though we don't always realize it, Earth's gravity pulls on us at all times. We need to exert energy just to move—just walking a few steps is in some ways a workout. But in space, with very little gravity, astronauts must make a special effort to stay healthy. They typically exercise for at least two hours per day, sometimes strapping themselves to treadmills to take a jog.

Why is it cold in space?

Heat and light come from stars. There are billions of stars in space, but they are very far apart. The places in between the stars have no light and no heat.

CRAZY!

Since there is no gravity in space, astronauts strap themselves into bed so they won't sleep-float. Sometimes they sleep in their seats or clip themselves to the wall. And yes, astronauts snore in space.

Why do some people believe that aliens built the pyramids in Egypt?

Since ancient civilizations didn't have modern machines, some people think the Great Pyramids—and many other complex structures around the world—were too difficult for people to build before machines were invented. Some think that aliens did the job. But most historians and engineers find it easier to believe that ancient people were stronger and smarter than we give them credit for.

Why are people who study aliens called UFOlogists?

The word comes from UFO, which stands for Unidentified Flying Object. Some people are certain they've seen UFOs, or that they exist. UFOlogists study all possible clues and evidence to support the idea that there are aliens out there and that they can be found.

OUTRAGEOUS!

Scientists have found forms of life in extreme temperatures deep in the ocean. If things can live under such extreme conditions on Earth, some scientists are hopeful that life forms may exist in other worlds, too.

Why do people listen to space?

Some people listen to space to search for evidence of aliens. And they are not alone! One project, called the Allen Telescope Array, will one day have 350 large radio dishes spread out across the Cascade Range of mountains in northern California. Each dish measures 19.5 feet (6 meters) across and is trained to search the night sky for radio signals that may be coming from distant civilizations. Is there anybody out there?

SCIENCE

Why are
**fireworks
different colors?**
Page 85

Why do some scientists work in special suits?

Scientists wear special suits to keep themselves safe in the lab. The safety gear they wear depends on what kind of work they do. Scientists who work with harmful chemicals or radiation wear suits that protect their skin. Scientists who encounter deadly fumes wear masks that control the air they breathe.

Why do some chemicals give off heat?

When chemicals are combined, they react with each other and change. Sometimes they create a third chemical that has less energy in it than the original two. When that happens, the extra energy has to go somewhere. Sometimes it's released as heat, sometimes as light, sometimes as gas, and sometimes … boom!

CRAZY !

A battery contains chemicals that can create electrical energy. In the 1700s, electricity was first captured in water-filled Leyden jars. It took several jars to hold a useful charge. These days, a single battery unit can power a flashlight.

Why do some **types of acid burn through metal?**

When acid is mixed with water, it releases a special type of hydrogen atom. This hydrogen atom reacts with the atoms in metal to make them dissolve. That's the "hole" story.

How is a **chemical compound different from a mixture?**

Think of it this way: Salt and pepper are a mixture. If you mix them up, you could (theoretically) separate them again. But mixing something like vinegar and baking soda forms a compound. The different parts of a compound are united all the way down to the level of their atoms. They're stuck together so well that they can't be separated into their original parts again—especially if they explode!

79

Why do **plants and animals have Latin names?**

Since the time of the Roman Empire, Greek and Latin were regularly taught in schools so that students could study classical literature in original texts. When scientists worldwide began to explore, organize, and name the natural world, they chose to use an international language: Latin. New plant and animal species are still assigned scientific names in Latin. Plants and animals have different common names in each language, but by sharing a Latin name, scientists can always communicate.

CRAZY !

Every living thing is made mostly of four basic elements: hydrogen, carbon, nitrogen, and oxygen. Of these, carbon is the only solid element. The rest are gases.

Why is **carbon so important to life?**

Things stay alive by converting fuel into energy. This requires a chemical reaction that always involves carbon. For example, plants combine the energy of the sun with carbon to produce the sugars they need to survive. Animals, including people, combine oxygen with the carbon in food (fats, proteins, and carbohydrates all contain carbon) to make energy.

Why does **every living thing have DNA?**

All living things are made up of cells. Complex plants and animals can each have billions or even trillions of cells, each with a specific job to do. DNA is the chemical that carries the structure for every living thing—a kind of code that tells each cell what to do. DNA is made up of genes that contain information that determines how living things act and appear. Each of your tiny cells has about six feet of DNA coiled inside of it.

Why does **mold grow on old food?**

Mold is a kind of fungus. Fungi reproduce by sending tiny seed-like spores into the air. These spores float around until they land on something they can grow on—like food. At first they're so tiny we can't see them, but as the food ages, the mold grows big and fuzzy so that we can see it—and steer clear!

Why do **echoes repeat?**

Sound travels in waves. An echo is what happens when loud
sound waves bounce off a hard object and bring the sound back
to you. To make an echo, it has to be quiet around you.
That's why you hear echoes in the mountains,
but not on busy city streets.

Why do compasses always point north?

Because the Earth has an iron core, its spinning creates a magnetic field. It's as if a giant magnet were buried in the center of the Earth, with the north and south poles as the tips. The needle of a compass is a small magnet balanced on a single point. Since the magnet in the compass always lines up with the Earth's magnetic field, one end always points north and the other always points south.

Why do we have seasons?

The Earth does not face the sun head-on. It's tilted. As the Earth orbits the sun, the angle of the tilt changes. When your half of the Earth is tilted away from the sun, it's winter. When it's tilted toward the sun, it's summer. Spring and fall occur halfway between each position.

Why are **lasers more powerful than other light beams?**

Regular light is made up of different colors that travel in different directions. Laser light is all one color that is super-focused and travels in the same direction. Since all the energy in a laser arrives in a very small area at the same time, laser light is far more powerful.

Light is a wave. Light is different colors. Light is little particles of energy, called photons. The speed of light is also the most basic unit of time. It may be called light, but it's got some heavy responsibilities!

COOL!

Why does **black light make some colors glow?**

Violet isn't actually at the bottom of the color spectrum. Black light produces ultraviolet light, a special light with a wavelength that's even shorter than violet light. Our eyes can't see ultraviolet light, but when it hits an object containing substances called phosphors, those phosphors glow. When a poster uses phosphorescent paint, it's the glow of the phosphors you see.

Why does a prism make a rainbow?

Regular light is a mix of red, orange, yellow, green, blue, indigo, and violet. A prism separates light into individual colors by bending the light as it passes through. Each color bends at a slightly different angle, so the colors are broken up and spread out to make a rainbow.

Why are fireworks different colors?

All fireworks contain gunpowder, which is what makes them burn and shoot up into the air. The colors in fireworks are produced by special chemicals that are packed in with the gunpowder. These chemical compounds burn in reds, greens, blues, and purples to make the colors we love to see light up the night sky.

Why are **super balls so bouncy?**

When rubber balls hit a hard surface, the rubber gets compressed, or flattened, at the point of impact. The ball naturally tries to get back to being round, so it pushes against the hard surface, causing it to bounce. A super ball is made of an especially hard, dense rubber that doesn't compress very much, so it doesn't need much energy to keep bouncing and bouncing and bouncing.

CRAZY!

Sound is made by vibrations. When something vibrates, it causes the air around it to move. When the vibrations are fast, you hear a high note. When the vibrations are slow, you hear a low note. These are sound waves. Make some waves!

Why do **people cry when they cut onions?**

Cutting onions releases a gas that mixes with the water that's naturally in our eyes. Together, they form an irritating chemical. Our eyes produce tears to wash it away.

How do **mirrors** reflect images?

Anything with a smooth surface that reflects light can be a mirror. A smooth surface is important because rough surfaces scatter light rather than reflect it. When light strikes the smooth surface of a mirror, it bounces back at the same angle. Your eyes see this reflected light as a mirror image. Mirrors today are usually made of clear glass coated with a thin layer of highly reflective metal, such as silver or aluminum.

Why do **some mints explode in cola?**

Cola is full of carbon dioxide gas, which makes it fizzy. In a glass, some of that gas escapes and forms foam, but most stays trapped in the liquid. Mints may look smooth, but they are actually covered with tiny bumps and pits. When you drop a mint in cola, bubbles stick to the bumps and pits and quickly rise to the surface, creating an explosion.

Why does **yeast make bread rise?**

Yeast is a tiny plant that digests flour and changes the flour's starch into sugar. Yeast then digests that sugar, turning it into alcohol and a gas called carbon dioxide (the same gas that's in soda pop). The bubbles of gas get trapped inside the dough. As the dough bakes, the gas bubbles break, leaving tiny air pockets in the dough that make it rise.

87

TECHNOLOGY

How do **touchscreens work?** Page 90

Why does **Wi-Fi** reach farther than **Bluetooth?**

Both use radio waves to connect devices. Bluetooth can only reach a small area using weak waves and can usually only connect to one device at a time. Wi-Fi networks (short for "wireless fidelity") have stronger waves that can reach farther and work with multiple devices at the same time.

OUTRAGEOUS!

A computer in your eyeglasses? Google is working on it! Users can take and share photos, video chat, and use the Internet. The device weighs about the same as sunglasses. Look out!

How do **touchscreens** work?

When your finger touches the electrodes that are set into a touchscreen, it completes a tiny electrical circuit. This circuit then activates a microcontroller that follows your finger's command. Try wearing rubber gloves. Most touchscreens won't work because electrical current can't pass through rubber.

Why are **hard drives** measured in MB, GB, or TB?

Computers store information in packets called *bytes*.
One byte is the size of one single letter or number, or a few dots. How many can a hard drive store? A megabyte (MB) is a million bytes, or roughly equivalent to a decent digital photo. A gigabyte (GB) is a billion bytes, or a good-quality movie. A terabyte (TB) is a trillion bytes, or a hard drive that holds a thousand movies. What's next? A petabyte.

How is **RAM memory different than hard drive memory?**

There are two types of memory in the computer: RAM (random access memory) is temporary, and hard drive memory is permanent. Think of RAM memory as the part of your mind that helps you do what you're doing right now. Hard drive memory is more like all of the memories you have stored. Each ability helps in different ways.

Why do **text messages and voice calls use data differently?**

Why are **broadcast antennas so tall?**

The tallest antennas are for AM radio stations, the oldest kind. AM radio waves can travel far, but buildings and other metal structures can easily block them. If the antennas were shorter, the radio waves couldn't reach your radio. Newer FM radio and TV signals travel more easily and only require the help of smaller antennas.

A text sends a small packet of data in one direction. A phone call transmits electronic voices in two directions. Texts create much smaller amounts of traffic on the network. A one-minute phone call requires more data than about 500 text messages, which is why texts cost much less to send.

Why do **many radios** stop working in tunnels?

For the most part, radio waves won't pass through solid matter such as the earth surrounding tunnels. Some tunnels, however, have transmitters that carry radio signals deep into the tunnel.

CRAZY!

If there are aliens out in space, they could listen to radio shows from long ago. TV and radio signals are still traveling through space, as are cell phone calls.

Why do **clocks** run clockwise?

Sundials, which measure time by the angle of shadows, were the original timepieces. Later, when clocks were first made, clockmakers copied the movement of the shadows. The first clockmakers were in the Northern Hemisphere, where the shadow on sundials moves to the right as the sun moves across the sky. That's why clocks, and the numbers on them, run "clockwise."

How does **technology help mend broken bones?**

Keeping a broken bone completely still by using a cast is the best way for it to heal. The first casts using bandages—soaked in plaster of Paris—were used in the 1850s. Today's casts are usually made of lightweight polyurethane, like the material that makes race cars. Doctors also use computer models to design plastic and metal cages like the one shown at left.

Why do **X-rays work?**

X-rays are a form of light that shines through soft things, such as skin and organs. The light does not pass well through harder body parts, like bones. When X-ray light shines through a body and onto a piece of film, it creates an image of the hard bones that the light can't shine through.

Why do **diabetics** often check their blood?

People with diabetes prick themselves several times a day with a small needle called a lancet. It checks the amount of sugar in their blood. Having the wrong level of blood sugar can become a serious problem. Scientists are working to develop new ways to keep tabs on sugar, using special tattoos, contact lenses, and skin patches . . . without the ouch!

Why can **surgeons do some operations without making big cuts?**

A device called a laparoscope lets surgeons see inside a patient through a tiny hole instead of a long cut. After making the small hole, the surgeon can put tools through the tube and fix whatever is wrong inside the patient. This kind of surgery can help people recover faster.

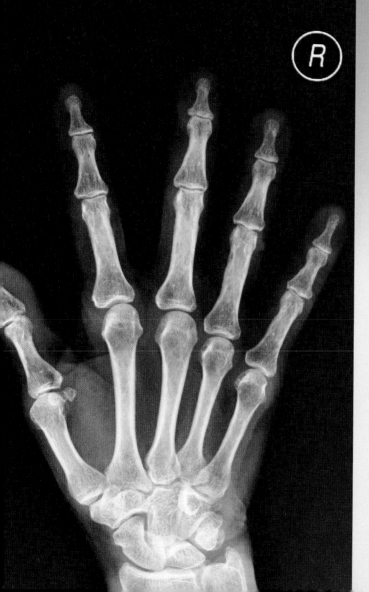

Why do police departments use robots?

Robots can go places that are not safe for human beings. Police departments can guide a special robot to investigate a suspicious package, or go into a building to search for people. The robot BOUNCE has cameras that snap pictures while its sensors detect air quality, temperature, and many hazards. This data is beamed back to mobile devices to give first responders a full picture of an emergency situation.

Why did scientists create a robot that can play soccer?

Scientists are designing a robot that can copy human movements. They chose soccer because the moves are complex and it's so popular around the world. CHARLI-2 is a full-size humanoid designed to run, kick, and balance, seeing the soccer field and opponents around it. Though CHARLI-2 is made of lightweight materials, it is still stiff and slow compared to human soccer stars.

Why is the Mars rover Curiosity unique among robots?

Many robots operate by remote control, but Curiosity set the record for distance. The rover responds to commands from drivers more than 60 million miles (97 million km) away! The commands take 10 to 20 minutes to reach the rover. Curiosity's battery allows it to travel longer than other rovers and its giant wheels help it roll over bigger obstacles.

CRAZY!

Thanks to robotic technology, some surgeons can operate on patients who are thousands of miles away. They use high-definition cameras and remote-operated instruments.

Why do students compete to build robots?

Each spring, thousands of students from around the world take part in a robotics competition called FIRST Robotics Competition. FIRST stands for For Inspiration and Recognition of Science and Technology. The competition helps kids get excited about science and technology. In just six weeks, they must build working robots that fight it out in different battle games.

Why is **China home to the highest bridges?**

Eight of the 12 highest bridges in the world are located in western China. The region's high mountains have forced engineers to come up with amazing ways to design bridges for railroads. The Sidu River Bridge, shown here, is the world's highest bridge. It sits 1,550 feet (472 m) above the Sidu River.

Why are **levees important?**

Cities that are built below the level of nearby water—ocean, lake, or river—are protected by levees (*leh*-vees). These high walls are made of earth or other strong materials. They prevent water from overflowing into the land where people are living, working, or farming. A protective network of floodwalls is critical for keeping some cities safe.

How do solar panels make electricity?

Energy from the sun usually turns into warmth on Earth. However, sunlight that hits a special cell in a solar panel turns that energy into electricity instead. The materials in the solar cells absorb the sunlight and react by making an electrical current. Solar cells are the key to harnessing solar power.

OUTRAGEOUS!

The sunlight that falls on a car creates more than enough energy to power it. Someday, solar panels may put an end to gas stations.

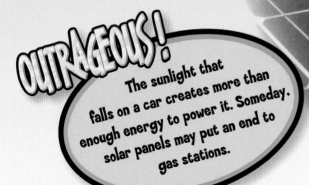

Why are some structures called green buildings?

Green buildings are environmentally friendly. They are built with materials that are recyclable or renewable. These energy-efficient homes and office buildings often use renewable energy sources, such as wind and sunlight, to help heat and cool them. In addition to helping the environment, green buildings help their owners save money on electric costs.

Why are so many tools inspired by space?

Cordless power tools, smoke detectors, speedy ear thermometers, scratch-proof glasses, high-tech sneaker insoles, and freeze-dried ice cream have one thing in common: they all came from research and development that began with NASA's space program. What's next? In 2012, NASA developed a space suit with flexible joints that protects users from radiation during long stays in space. What use could it have here on Earth?

Why is GPS so smart?

The Global Positioning System, or GPS, uses satellites to find locations. The satellites receive a signal from a GPS device or cell phone. The device locates four or more satellites near it, calculates its distance to each, and uses the information to locate the GPS user at that moment. GPS receivers can also calculate speed, distance, and directions.

Why does it take so long **to get to Mars?**

Mars is about 60 million miles (97 million km) from Earth. The distance varies, because the two planets orbit the sun at different rates. Even using the fastest spacecraft humans have ever made it still takes more than 150 days to reach the Red Planet.

Why is **SpaceShipTwo out of this world?**

SpaceShipTwo was the first ship to sell tickets for a ride to space. On April 29, 2013, the craft had its first powered test flight. Next up: taking tourists on suborbital flights. That means the ship goes straight up, about 62 miles (100 km) into space. After about six minutes of weightless floating, the passengers and the ship come back to Earth.

Why is **the Hubble telescope unique?**

The Hubble telescope has been spinning in space since 1990, orbiting the Earth and sending back images from far, far, away. From it we've learned, for instance, how old the universe is (13.7 billion years) and that tiny Pluto has three even-tinier moons. There are other space telescopes, but only Hubble can be repaired

TRANSPORTATION

Why are some trucks in Australia so long? Page 109

ROAD TRAIN

Why don't **hang gliders need engines?**

First, you launch from a hill, or you're towed by a motor vehicle—maybe a boat or an airplane. Then you cut loose. The hang glider floats on cushions of warm air that rise up from the ground. Gliders also use the wind that is created when air moves against mountains. To steer, you move your body around.

CRAZY!

With the invention of jet airplanes in the 1940s, aircraft could fly faster than the speed of sound—about 750 mph (1,207 kph). In 1947, U.S. Air Force pilot Chuck Yeager became the first person to break this barrier.

Why do **helicopters move in so many directions?**

Unlike an airplane's fixed wings, the blades of a helicopter can be adjusted separately. The main rotor blade provides lift as the blades rotate. The helicopter pilot can change the angle of each blade to make the craft move in any direction.

Why are **hot air balloons hard to steer?**

Balloons do not have engines or propellers, so they must move in whatever direction the wind blows. Pilots can't direct the balloon by themselves, except to go up or down to take advantage of the shifting wind. To rise, pilots turn up the propane burners that power the balloon. To drop, they turn down the heat.

Why are **some planes "invisible" to radar?**

Radar works by sending out radio signals that bounce off objects. The radar operator reads the signals that bounce back to detect where an airplane might be. Some stealth planes are coated with special coverings that absorb these radio waves and have many flat surfaces or sharp angles to deflect, rather than reflect, the waves.

Why can't **giant blimps carry many passengers?**

Blimps are massive, but most of their bulk is filled with the gases that keep them afloat. The only place available for passengers on most blimps is in a small cabin underneath, called a gondola. The famous Goodyear blimp, for example, can carry only two pilots and six passengers.

Why are engines measured in horsepower?

James Watt, who invented the modern steam engine in the 1760s, also came up with the idea of horsepower. He used it to compare the work done by his new engine to the work done by the horses his engine would replace. Horsepower measures the work done by one horse, usually in one minute. It now measures performance for all types of engines.

CRAZY!

In 1997, Andy Green set a land-speed record for a car: 764 mph (1,230 kph). Now he's shooting to beat 1,000 mph (1,609 kph), at the wheel of the BLOODHOUND SSC. Start your engines!

Why were early cars called horseless carriages?

In the late 1800s, when cars were invented, most people traveled in carriages that were pulled by horses. The design of early cars looked much like traditional carriages . . . but got their power from engines rather than animals.

Why are **electric cars so quiet?**

Electric cars run on the same kind of battery that laptop computers use. Most cars use gas engines that make a lot of noise, but the electric motor is nearly silent. These quiet, clean, battery-powered vehicles can be charged using a standard wall plug. The Tesla (left) is extremely fast and powerful for an electric car.

Why are **race cars built so low to the ground?**

By making the cars as low as possible, designers increase the "downforce" on a car. Downforce is the pressure of air racing over the car, which presses it down on the track. Low car design prevents most of the air from going underneath, which would create lift. Strong downforce helps the driver keep up speed as the car tears up the turns.

Why are motorcycles sometimes called hogs?

In the 1920s, a group of motorcycle racers had a pet hog for a mascot. They carried the hog on a motorcycle during a victory lap. The team was called the hog boys, and their motorcycles were known as hogs. Originally, just Harley-Davidson bikes were called hogs, but now the term describes any large, powerful motorcycle.

Why do some motorcycles have spikes on their tires?

Designed for racing on ice, special motorcycles have spiked tires to help grip the slippery surface. Some dirt bike tires also have deep, spiky treads to help grip the trail.

Why are some trucks in Australia so long?

When a truck is pulling four or five trailers, it's called a road train. They are perfect for the Outback in Australia, which has many long, straight roads that stretch over long distances. These mega-trucks don't have to make sharp turns, and they save gas. Legally, they can stretch to 175.5 ft (53.5 m). However, one record-breaking truck pulled 113 trailers, measuring 4,837 ft (1474 m).

COOL!

Some electric skateboards can move faster than 20 mph (33 kph). Some models have off-road tires for dirt and beach use.

Why can cable cars only move along certain streets?

Cable cars, such as those used in San Francisco, California, don't have a motor. They are powered by the pull of a steel cable, like a bike chain, that moves beneath the street. Unlike other vehicles, cable cars can't move from street to street, but can only go along routes where cables have been installed.

Why are gondolas used in Venice?

Long, narrow boats called gondolas were designed more than 1,000 years ago to navigate the many canals of Venice. No cars can drive in this waterlogged Italian city, so people rely on boats to get around. Gondolas are used privately, or as water-taxis, like those that ferry passengers across the Grand Canal, the longest waterway in Venice. The sleek design of these boats allows the pilot, or gondolier, to steer through some 150 narrow canals and under ancient bridges.

Why did old-time sailing ships need so much rope?

All the ropes on a sailboat are called rigging. Large sailing ships with three masts can set more than a dozen different sails at the same time—and each sail needs several ropes to control it from the deck. Other ropes were used to hold the masts steady or haul up the yards, which are large wooden crosspieces.

Why do **most rowers face backward?**

Rowing with your back to the front of the boat is easier. Although you can't see exactly where you're going, rowing that way lets you give more power to the oars by using your back and legs. That's where your biggest muscles are. Try it both ways to see for yourself!

OUTRAGEOUS!

At 590 feet (180 m) long, the Azzam is the world's largest yacht. Launched in 2013, it's the latest ultra-massive, ultra-luxury ship. By the time you read this, there will probably be a bigger one.

How can **little tugboats pull such large loads?**

Tugboats are quite a bit smaller than the huge ships they guide. But looks can be deceiving: they have massive, powerful engines. The small boats can create huge pushing or pulling power with steady work from their onboard diesel power plants.

Why can **some subs sink to the world's deepest places?**

Deep-diving craft are called submersibles. A few have gone 6.8 miles (11 km) below the surface of the sea to explore Earth's deepest point—the Pacific's Marianas Trench. Submersibles have very thick metal hulls that can withstand the enormous pressure of deep waters. They have to be small —only a couple of crew members can make each dive.

Why are subs faster underwater than above it?

The streamline shape of a submarine lets it move more easily when it is entirely submerged in water. This wasn't always true. Older subs, such as those from World War II, did the opposite— they were designed to be faster on the surface than below it.

CRAZY !

In 1958, the U.S. nuclear submarine Nautilus became the first to complete a voyage beneath the Arctic ice at the North Pole.

Why do submarines use sonar?

How do you steer a submarine? Subs don't have windows because the intense pressure underwater would break them. Besides, there's no light down below. Subs can't use radar because radio waves don't travel well underwater. Sound, however, travels very well in water. Sonar transmits a pulse of sound into the water and measures how long it takes to bounce off another object. The echoes of sound help submariners determine what objects are around them.

Why is sub grub special?

Serving in a sub is difficult work—sailors spend weeks or months in a small, windowless space without fresh air. To compensate, the U.S. Navy serves these sailors food that's more interesting than the grub on other ships. Submariners also eat four meals per day: the usual three, plus midnight rations. Some subs serve freshly baked bread every day, giving new meaning to the idea of submarine sandwiches.

Why do submariners wear sneakers?

Staying quiet underwater is very important for submarines, since stealth helps them stay hidden from enemies. Wearing sneakers or other soft-bottomed shoes helps the sailors inside the subs stay quiet when moving around.

Why are
some bikes called fixies?

Fixies are fixed gear bikes that have only one gear. They can not coast—the rider must pedal constantly. Fixies also let you ride backwards. Most fixies have very thin tires and only a front brake.

CRAZY!

Each year, groups of college engineering students build canoes and race them. So what's unusual? The canoes are made entirely of concrete!

Why do monster trucks have transparent floors?

Monster trucks are usually pickup trucks with super-large wheels. Their main tasks include looking cool, winning tug-of-war contests, and crushing cars. The cab might be as high as 15 feet (4.6m) off the ground, which means the driver can't see what's directly in front of the truck. The clear floor beneath the driver's feet makes it easier to see what's coming near—and under—its wheels.

Why don't some trains need drivers?

Thanks to computers, driverless trains, like some used for airport shuttles, can be run by remote control. Operators at a central station command the trains to stop and go along their short routes. Cameras help the operators keep an eye on platforms and rail lines. Stand clear of the closing doors!

How do street luges go so fast?

It used to be called "laying down on your skateboard." When the skateboards got bigger, they got a new name: street luge. Because riders are very low to the ground, a street luge has very little air resistance. Drivers can position their body to slice cleanly through the air as they barrel down steep tracks. Without any sort of motor, they rely on gravity to reach speeds of more than 90 mph (145 kph). Warning: do not try this at home!

U.S. HISTORY

Why is December 7, 1941,
"a date which will live in infamy?"
Page 128

Why did early explorers call native people Indians?

Sometimes a mistake just won't go away. In 1492, when Christopher Columbus sailed the ocean blue, he was looking for a trade route to India. Something got in his way—the Western Hemisphere. When Columbus landed in the Americas, he believed he was in Asia. He met the natives and called them "Indians." He wasn't in India, but the name stuck.

Why are feathers symbolic to Native Americans?

Though different tribes have given feathers different meanings, to be honored with a feather means a great deal. Feathers are symbols of strength, honor, wisdom, and power. The greatest reward is often the feather of an eagle, which is said to be the leader of all birds. Ornate feather headdresses and costumes are worn with great pride and respect.

Why is **face paint important to Native American culture?**

Western artists—from painters to movie-makers—often show native people wearing war paint. It is said that some designs have protective powers, while others make warriors look more fierce. Face paint is sometimes worn like a prize medal, in rituals and ceremonies, or as camouflage. It also offers the skin protection from harsh sun and wind.

Why do **tribes hold pow-wows?**

The actual word is *pau-wau*, and it's a special tribal ceremony. Many tribes have long had these spiritual ceremonies to celebrate life, honor death, act out stories, give thanks for a good hunt or harvest, or to prepare for battle. A pau-wau may be a private event or a show for visitors, and it can include dancing, drumming, singing, or chanting.

COOL!

Totem poles were created by the tribes of the Pacific Northwest. The animals and other symbols carved into the tall trees are not mystical or religious symbols. Instead, totem poles are designed to pass along stories of the tribe, family, or person who did the carving.

Why do we say Christopher Columbus discovered America?

Columbus never actually reached mainland North America, but his crew did visit many Caribbean islands, with short stops in South America and Central America. So, technically, Columbus was the first European explorer to find and chart a route to the Americas. The first beach in the Americas that Columbus landed on was in the Bahamas. The last was Jamaica, where he was stranded for a year before finally returning to Spain.

CRAZY !

The Mayflower originally had a sister ship, the Speedwell, along on their historic journey. The smaller Speedwell started leaking immediately. Some Speedwell passengers crowded onto the Mayflower. The rest went back to England.

Why do we call the Plymouth settlers Pilgrims?

The word *pilgrim* means a person who travels to a foreign land. In 1620, a ship called the *Mayflower* set sail from Plymouth, England. After 66 days at sea, the 102 passengers on board reached what's now called Plymouth, Massachusetts. The early colonists were members of a strict religious group called Puritans. They left Europe so they could practice their religion in their own way. Plymouth became the second permanent British colony in the New World.

Why is Jamestown, Virginia sometimes called America's birthplace?

Jamestown was the first British colony in what became the United States. In 1607, 105 passengers on three British ships came to live in the New World. The colony immediately struggled against bad weather, starvation, and most importantly, the local Powhatan inhabitants. Many settlers died, but the survivors kept the colony going.

Why were the **thirteen American colonies so heavily taxed?**

The year 1763 marked the end of seven years of fighting between France and Britain. After the signing of the Treaty of Paris, France gave its North American settlements to Britain, which wanted its colonies to help pay for their protection, among other things. Taxes are the most direct way for a government to raise money.

Why did **George Washington's army cross the Delaware River?**

It's a famous scene: Washington standing in a rowboat on a cold night. But why? Because Washington was desperate. The war was going badly. New York had fallen. Philadelphia was endangered. The British seemed to have all the advantages, which is why their army was relaxing in Trenton, New Jersey, on Christmas night of 1776. When more than 5,000 of Washington's soldiers snuck across the freezing Delaware River to capture the British troops, it was a much-needed and unconventional victory for the colonies.

CRAZY!

Thousands of German soldiers fought for the British. They were mercenaries —soldiers for hire, who are in it for the money.

Why did **some French soldiers fight in the American Revolutionary War?**

It's called the American Revolution, but it was actually a mini-World War. In order to gain independence from Britain, the U.S. badly needed an ally with ships, soldiers, and money. Ben Franklin and Thomas Jefferson, among others, persuaded French King Louis XVI to sign a treaty in 1778. The treaty joined the countries as allies against Britain. France's help was critical to America winning the war.

Why did **the battle at Yorktown help end the Revolutionary War?**

In 1781, there were strong doubts about an American victory. That summer, the British army had set up camp in Yorktown, Virginia, to wait for supply ships. Yorktown is a peninsula, surrounded by water on three sides, which leaves only one way out by land. American and French soldiers strategically cut off any possibility of a land escape. No British ships arrived. On October 19, 1781, after the short battle of Yorktown, the trapped British army surrendered and the war was essentially won.

123

Why was the Civil War the bloodiest war in our nation's history?

Of all the wars U.S. soldiers have fought in, none has cost more American lives than the Civil War, which was fought from 1861 to 1865. The reason is simple: soldiers fighting on both sides, North and South, were American. Historians estimate between 650,000 and 750,000 American war deaths. In 1860, the U.S. population was just more than 31 million, which means that about 2 percent of the whole population—1 in 50 people—died during the war.

Why was it called the Civil War?

The war between the states had many names. The North called it, among other things, the War for the Union and the War of the Rebellion. The South referred to it by names including the War of Secession, the War for Southern Independence, and the War of Northern Aggression. Officially, it is called the Civil War, the name given to any war fought by two groups from the same country.

OUTRAGEOUS!

Though the North called themselves "Union" and the South "Confederates," the words actually mean the same thing: a group or organization working together for the same purpose.

Why do many Civil War battles have two different names?

Traditionally, the U.S. military chooses the name of a battle. In the case of the Civil War, each side picked a name. The North tended to name battles after nearby geography, such as lakes or hills. The South preferred to name battles for a nearby town or manmade landmark. For example, what the North called the Battle of Bull Run—a stream— the South called Manassas, which was a railroad station. The Battle of Ball's Bluff, a hill, was referred to in the South as Leesburg.

Why did slaves fight for the South?

After President Abraham Lincoln signed the Emancipation Proclamation in 1863, 180,000 slaves were inspired to join the Northern army to fight for freedom. But some Southern slaveholders forced thousands of slaves to help in the fight. Many were assigned roles as servants, cooks, laborers, musicians, and guards. Occasionally, some slaves served as soldiers in combat.

Why were the Monitor and the Merrimack famous ships?

The North's Monitor and the South's Merrimack, (a 4,636-ton steamship that was later renamed Virginia) were the first armored, ironclad ships to battle each other. Heavy and ugly and slow, both were covered in so much iron they could hardly maneuver. Few shots were fired during their famous battle on March 9, 1862, at Hampton Roads, Virginia. The Monitor was disabled but not destroyed—a victory for the South.

How did toys help the Wright Brothers fly?

The Wright brothers, Orville and Wilbur, were determined to unlock the mysteries of flight. They studied kites and how they rode the wind. They looked at how gliders could be steered through the sky. Finally, the brothers built different versions of an engine-powered airplane using bicycle parts, among other things. On December 17, 1903, their plane, called the *Wright Flyer*, got off the ground. Though it stayed in the air for just 12 seconds, it was one of the most famous flights in history.

Why did George Washington Carver experiment with peanuts?

Carver was born a slave in the 1860s. After he was set free, he put his scientific skills to work to help poor farmers, especially in the South. These farmers needed to expand from planting only cotton to growing a variety of crops, which is an important way to keep soil healthy. Peanuts were an excellent choice, but there wasn't enough demand to make them profitable to plant. Carver discovered more than 300 uses for peanuts—including paints, bleach, shampoo, ink, fuel, and of course, peanut butter.

Why could **Henry Ford** make so many more cars than his competitors?

Cars were built expensively, one at a time, until Henry Ford found a way to make more of them without increasing their cost. His assembly line's relatively inexpensive mass production revolutionized car manufacturing. It also changed life in the U.S. forever. Released in 1908, Ford's Model T was an instant hit. It cost $850, about half the usual price at the time.

Why did **Samuel Morse** develop the telegraph?

In 1825, before there were telephones, news traveled very slowly. By the time the painter Samuel Morse heard that his wife was dying, he was too far away to reach her in time to say goodbye. Morse vowed not to let that happen to other people. Early telegraphs already existed, but by 1840, Morse invented a signal that could travel across large distances. He also created a coded alphabet of dots and dashes to send and receive messages, named Morse Code in his honor.

Why did World War II break out?

It's complicated, but the wheels for World War II were set in motion when Germany lost World War I in 1918. The Germans had to pay very expensive war costs, which made Germany a poor country. Many Germans were so angry about bad postwar conditions, they helped bring Nazi leader Adolf Hitler to power in 1933. Hitler and the Nazi Party began a reign of terror. In 1939, Hitler led the country into World War II. The terrible war did not end until 1945.

CRAZY!

The sturdy Jeep got its start in World War II. The military vehicle was officially called a "general purpose" vehicle, or G.P. for short. Later, when civilian models were sold, they were called "Jeeps."

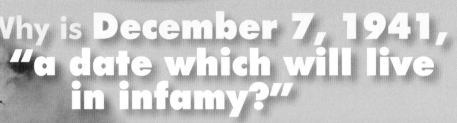

Why is December 7, 1941, "a date which will live in infamy?"

On that sunny morning, the skies above Pearl Harbor, in Hawaii, were darkened by the approach of about 350 Japanese airplanes. U.S. Navy ships in the harbor were attacked. More than 3,600 Americans were killed or injured in the surprise attack, making it the biggest foreign attack on U.S. soil to date. The next day, President Roosevelt called the attack "a date which will live in infamy," and U.S. forces joined the fight in World War II.

Why was the Normandy invasion called D-Day?

By 1944, the U.S. and its allies were gaining strength in Europe. The plan was to invade the French beach at Normandy, then drive the Germans out of France and other countries. Only the top generals knew when this invasion of 160,000 troops would take place. Speaking in code, they agreed the invasion would happen on D-Day, at H-Hour and M-Minute. That turned out to be June 6, 1944, at 6:30 a.m. The successful attack was a critical turning point in the war.

Why did the war in Europe end before the war in the Pacific?

There were two major battlefronts during World War II—the war against Germany and Italy in Europe, and the war against Japan in the Pacific. Adolf Hitler killed himself on April 30, 1945. All of his armies surrendered by May 8, which is referred to as V-E Day, for Victory in Europe. The fighting in Japan ended on August 14, 1945, which is referred to as V-J Day.

Why were U.S. soldiers called G.I.s?

During World War II, anything the U.S. government made—from shoes to guns to chocolate—was known as "government issue," or "G.I." Some American soldiers played off the term and unofficially called themselves G.I.s. Later, G.I. Joe soldier dolls became one of the most popular toys in the country.

Why did the Cold War lead to the space race?

For almost 50 years after World War II, the U.S. and the U.S.S.R. were bitter enemies. That period is known as the Cold War, because the two enemies didn't fight with weapons. The rivals also competed in a space race starting around 1957, when the Soviet Union launched *Sputnik 1*, the first satellite.

Why was a dog sent into space?

In the early days of the space race, scientists did not know what would happen to a living being beyond earth's atmosphere. The Soviet Union experimented with a former stray dog named Laika, which means "barker" in Russian. Laika was trained to ride in a rocket before she blasted into orbit in a pressurized cabin aboard *Sputnik II* on November 3, 1957. The beloved canine cosmonaut did not survive the mission.

Why did the first U.S. space missions have Latin names?

Beginning in 1959, NASA led the American space program. Their first major mission, Project Mercury, was named for the Roman god of speed. Next came Project Gemini, which is the Latin word for twins. Why twins? Because, for the first time, there would be two crewmen aboard. The moon missions were named the Apollo project in honor of the Roman god of the sun.

COOL!

In 1969, American astronauts Neil Armstrong and Buzz Aldrin landed on the moon in a lunar module like this one. They planted a waving flag — but there is no wind on the moon. The metal flag was made to look like it's fluttering.

Why are Yuri Gagarin and Neil Armstrong space pioneers?

Both men were the first to set records in space. Soviet cosmonaut Yuri Gagarin (right) was the first person to orbit the Earth. He flew aboard the *Vostok 1*, circling the Earth once on April 12, 1961. Eight years later, on July 20, 1969, during the Apollo 11 mission, U.S. astronaut Neil Armstrong became the first person to walk on the moon.

Why did Dr. Martin Luther King Jr. give his "I Have a Dream" speech?

On August 28, 1963, Martin Luther King Jr. spoke before a crowd of 250,000 people in Washington, D.C. The historic event, called the March on Washington, was a rally calling for civil rights, jobs, and general equality for African Americans. The march ended at the Lincoln Memorial, where Dr. King gave one of the greatest speeches in U.S. history. The powerful energy of the event strongly influenced lawmakers to pass the 1964 Civil Rights Act and the 1965 Voting Rights Act.

Why did saying "no" make Rosa Parks famous?

Rosa Parks (wearing glasses at left) made history by sitting where she wanted to on a public bus in Montgomery, Alabama. In 1955, laws in some states required separate seating for black and white passengers. Parks, a black woman, was arrested for not giving her seat to a white man. Her arrest led to a 381-day bus boycott throughout Montgomery. The U.S. Supreme Court outlawed separate seating on buses in 1956. Parks' courageous act was an important step in the American Civil Rights movement.

Why was the War in Vietnam so widely protested?

From the 1950s until 1975, the U.S. fought against communist North Vietnam. The U.S. feared the spread of communism, but millions opposed involvement in this complex war, which seemed to have no clear purpose. Hundreds of thousands of young American men were drafted and sent to fight in Vietnam. More than 1 million people died in the war, including some 58,000 U.S. soldiers. People marched, attended rallies, and wrote protest songs calling for the end of what they saw as an unjust war.

Why is **a famous political scandal named for a hotel?**

When President Richard M. Nixon ran for re-election in 1972, workers for his re-election campaign broke into rivals' offices at the Watergate hotel and office building in Washington, D.C. Five men were arrested trying to hide microphones inside the rival Democratic Party headquarters. The arrest, and the ways the White House tried to cover it up, revealed a much larger web of scandal that landed many of Nixon's top officials in jail. Investigators charged Nixon with abusing power to hide the crime. He resigned from office in 1974.

CRAZY!

President Gerald Ford is the only person ever to become president without having been elected as either president or vice president. First, Ford was appointed to replace Vice President Spiro Agnew, who resigned amid scandal in 1973. Then, he became president when Richard Nixon resigned in 1974.

WORLD HISTORY

Why did **Vikings give New York its name?** Page 147

Why are these called the Seven Wonders of the Ancient World?

More than 2,000 years ago, these were the top seven amazing structures that world travelers tried to see. The wonders (and the travelers) encircled the Mediterranean Sea.

Lighthouse of Alexandria

Location: Alexandria, Egypt
Built: 280 B.C.
Destroyed: by earthquakes in 1323 A.D.
Why Wonder-ful: Built 450 feet (137 m) high in the days before cranes, the lighthouse signaled from Pharos Island to ships and travelers as far as 35 miles (56 km) away.

Tomb of Maussolios at Halicarnassus

Location: Southwest Turkey
Built: 350 B.C.
Destroyed: By earthquakes in 1494 A.D.
Why Wonder-ful: The 135-foot-high (41-m) mega-tomb of Persian King Maussolios, which was covered in sculpted images, gave us the word "mausoleum."

Great Pyramid of Giza

Location: Cairo, Egypt
Built: 2560 B.C.
Destroyed: Wasn't!
Why Wonder-ful: At 480 feet (146 m), made of more than 2 million two-ton (1.8-tonne) stones, the picturesque pyramid was the world's tallest structure for nearly 4,000 years.

CRAZY!

You could only visit all Seven Wonders for about 50 years, until the Colossus of Rhodes was toppled by an earthquake in 226 B.C.

Temple of Artemis at Ephesus

Location: Selcuk, Turkey
Built: 550 B.C.
Destroyed: Twice, by invaders, in 356 B.C. and 262 A.D.

Why Wonder-ful: More than 120 pure marble columns, each 60 feet (18 m) high, supported this massive indoor temple full of art and sculpture.

Hanging Gardens of Babylon

Location: Al-Hillah, Iraq
Built: 600 B.C.
Destroyed: Perhaps by an earthquake in 1–100 B.C.

Why Wonder-ful: These mountain-size, lush, manmade gardens provided a brilliant irrigation system, not to mention they smelled great!.

Colossus at Rhodes

Location: Rhodes, Greece
Built: 280 B.C.
Destroyed: By earthquake in 226 B.C.

Why Wonder-ful: The 100-foot (30-m) statue towered over a harbor entrance. Though it was built 2,000 years before the Statue of Liberty, it was nearly as tall.

Statue of Zeus

Location: Olympia, Greece
Built: 450 B.C.
Destroyed: By unknown causes in 400-500 A.D.

Why Wonder-ful: The seated statue of Zeus boasted 40 feet (12 m) of ivory, gold, and jewels.

Why was King Tut called the Boy King?

More than 3,000 years ago, King Tutankhamun took the throne when he was just 9 years old. King Tut, as he is called, ruled for half his life, with the help of many generals and advisors. His historic life ended at the age of 19. The boy (and teen) king's mummy was discovered in 1922. Though many thought he'd been murdered, scientists now believe he died of complications from malaria and a broken leg.

COOL !

Queen Hathepeshut was one of the most accomplished pharaohs. She ruled for about 22 years—a very long and successful reign for a pharaoh.

Why did the great pyramids have fake entrances?

Two words: grave robbers. Since the pharaohs packed their tombs for the afterlife, everyone knew the pyramids were big, pointy treasure chests. A grand entrance was carved into the side of a pyramid. That was a dead end— sometimes literally, when guards were on duty. The real doors were hidden among the stones.

Why was Cleopatra the last pharaoh of Egypt?

Cleopatra VII Philopator reigned over Egypt for 21 years, from 51 to 30 B.C. The powerful queen became the sole ruler in 47 B.C., at the age of 21. She won the hearts of two powerful Roman leaders, Julius Caesar and Mark Antony. At the time, Rome and Egypt were rivals. She took her own life at age 39. As she had no children to succeed her, the reign of pharaohs ended. Soon after her death, the Romans took control of Egypt. Cleopatra's story of love, power, and defeat has fascinated people for thousands of years.

Why is the Sphinx a symbol of Egypt?

The Sphinx, a lion with a human head, was believed to have divine power. Ancient Egyptians built many sphinx statues. This one, Egypt's Great Sphinx of Giza, is the world's largest, measuring 66 feet (20 m) high and 241 feet (73 m) long. Many historians believe the roughly 4,500-year-old big cat was built to guard the Great Pyramids that stand right behind it. The sandstone monument was buried under sand for many centuries. Over time, water and pollution have chipped away at its surface.

Why was **Alexander the Great so great?**

This student of the Greek philosopher Aristotle became a brilliant general and one of the mightiest conquerors in history. His empire stretched from Greece to Egypt to India. In 332 B.C. he founded Alexandria, Egypt's second largest city. By the age of 30, he united Greece, then spread Greek culture to much of the world. He died of malaria at age 33, but the dynasty he began ruled for 300 years.

What was the **Pax Romana?**

Pax Romana is Latin for "Roman peace." This term describes about 200 years of general peace in the Roman Empire, from 27 B.C. to 180 A.D. During the Pax Romana, the Roman Empire reached its peak. Romans brought high-tech roads, sewers, and aqueducts to carry fresh water to the lands they conquered. This earned them good will. But much of the credit for the "pax" goes to the many Roman soldiers who made sure that peace reigned.

Why is **Greece known as the birthplace of democracy?**

Early Greeks believed in government by the people, trial by jury, and equality under the law. Ancient Athens was then a separate city-state but is now the capital of Greece. It was the first known government to have a way for people to vote directly. Five hundred citizens were selected to create the laws. Then, citizens voted on these laws. This experiment became a working model for democracy today.

Why was **Roman entertainment called a circus?**

Don't think of clowns and balancing acts. In this case, *circus*, the Latin word for circle, describes the huge, nearly round open-air arenas where Romans held chariot races, gladiator battles, and other big events. Circuses were one of the main entertainments of the time.

OUTRAGEOUS!

Before Julius and Augustus Caesar became Roman emperors, there were only 10 months in a calendar year. In 45 B.C., the Julian calendar introduced the concept of leap year, and added two more months. Can you guess which ones?

Why are **long races called marathons?**

Marathon is a city in Greece. During a battle there in 490 B.C., Athens defeated Persia. According to either history or legend, a messenger named Pheidippides ran directly from Marathon to Athens, a distance of about 25 miles (40 km), to spread the news of the great victory. He then dropped dead on the spot. Marathons returned with the first modern Olympics, held in Athens, Greece, in 1896. Modern marathons run slightly longer, measuring 26.2 miles (42.195 km).

Why was Moctezuma such a respected Aztec leader?

If you thought the famous Aztec emperor was called Montezuma, now you know his real name. From 1440 until his death in 1469, Moctezuma I expanded his Aztec empire through Mexico and Central America. He became the leader of an alliance between the Aztec, the Texcoco, and the Tlacopan peoples. His successful reign brought unprecedented power and influence to the Aztec empire.

CRAZY!

The Aztecs didn't call themselves "Aztec." They referred to themselves as the Mexica people. That's where Mexico got its name.

Why did the Maya make human sacrifices?

More than 1,000 years ago, the Maya built a thriving civilization in Central America and southern Mexico. They built grand palaces, temples, and pyramids, and created intricate art. The Maya sacrificed human blood as an offering to their gods. This was their most serious way to ask for a favor: to win a war, to end sickness or drought, or to honor a king. There were special altars and tools for the job. If being chosen for sacrifice was an honor—it probably didn't feel that way!

Why did **the Aztecs take games so seriously?**

In the 1400s, the Aztecs ruled much of Mexico and Central America. But they still found time for sports. The 3,000-year-old game of Ollamaliztli was an Aztec invention. Think soccer plus basketball—players kicked or threw a heavy rubber ball through stone rings. Athletes wore leather pads to protect them during the action, and legend has it that losers lost more than the game. They were beheaded.

Why didn't **the Aztec empire last very long?**

The Aztec empire was an advanced culture with its own philosophy, science, architecture, strength, and great wealth. The empire did not rise until the 1300s, and it was thriving by the time another empire came to town: the Spanish, with their guns. The Spanish arrived on ships in the 1500s, seeking gold, slaves, and land. Since the Aztecs had everything except the guns, their empire quickly fell.

Why was the
Silk Road so important?

The Silk Road is the name of the ancient trade route that connected Europe and Asia. Before there were trains and planes, merchants traveled along the Silk Road to trade goods, including porcelain, gold, ivory, spices, and, of course, silk. Since before 100 B.C., travelers on the Silk Road carried much more than goods. Language, culture, religion, art, and literature were shared. Cities along the route became centers where people could trade ideas and share their customs.

Why is
China called
the Middle Kingdom?

In China, people call their country by these Chinese letters, pronounced *zhong guo*, which means Middle Kingdom. The land was (and is) so large, the ancient Chinese believed they were in the middle of the whole civilized world.

中国

Why are so
many people
followers of Confucius?

Confucius, who lived from 551 to 479 B.C., was ancient China's most famous teacher. He advised princes that to win people's loyalty, a ruler must be fair. His messages focused on the most proper and compassionate ways for people to act at home, in public, and in politics. His teachings taught peace in violent times to many millions of people. Confucianism is still widely followed today. "To learn and to apply what one has learned—isn't that a pleasure?" is one of his famous sayings.

Why was **Genghis Khan** called the **Universal Ruler?**

Genghis Khan came from Mongolia, which is now in Northern China. Around 1175 A.D., at the age of 20, the warrior gathered a great army that conquered and united most of Asia. Because he was the leader of their leaders, his subjects called him Universal Ruler. At the time, Khan's Mongol empire became the largest empire the world had ever seen.

Who was **Chairman Mao?**

COOL!

Paper was invented during China's Han Dynasty, around 105 A.D. The Chinese also invented ink, the compass, and silk.

In 1949, Mao Zedong, head of China's Communist Party, changed China from a country of rich landowners and peasant farmers to a country governed by communism. With communism, a country's resources are shared, the government controls all property, and many freedoms are restricted. His Great Leap Forward was an attempt to modernize his rural country by building cities and factories, relocating people, controlling farming, and much more. Mao's plan to change China's economy and farming system failed, and millions died of starvation.

Why were books rare in the Middle Ages?

Relatively few books were produced during the Middle Ages because the modern printing press had not yet been invented. Books—handmade by monks and other scholars—were mostly bibles and other religious texts. These were often beautiful works of art, with elegant lettering, brightly colored illustrations, and pages that were sewn into a leather cover by hand. Fast work? Hardly. Especially at a time when very few people could read.

COOL!

The word "medieval" comes from medium aevum, which is Latin for middle age.

Why did knights often wear feathers on their helmets?

It's hard to identify your allies when you're fighting in full armor. Knights and other soldiers wore large, colored feathers, or plumes, on top of their helmets so they could quickly tell friend from enemy. During jousts and friendly contests, knocking off another person's plume with your weapon often made you the winner.

Why are **there so many different titles for royalty?**

How do you know who's who in European royalty? A title indicates a person's closeness to the throne. It once defined how much land and how many subjects he or she ruled. The most common titles, in order of superiority, are emperor, king/queen, prince/princess, duke/duchess, marquis/marquise, count/countess, baron/baroness, and knight.

Why are **they called the Middle Ages?**

The period in Europe we call the Middle Ages was the era of knights and monks and the black plague. It got its name by coming between two eras that had more scientific and artistic advances. This 1,000-year period began when the Roman Empire fell, around the fifth century. It wasn't until the Renaissance, in the 15th century, that Europe came out of its slow middle years, and the Middle Ages reached their end.

Why did **Vikings give New York its name?**

It takes a village to name a city. The Dutch colony of New Amsterdam was renamed New York, in honor of the Duke of York, when the British took control of it in 1664. York is a walled city in the North Yorkshire region of England. York was the English version of Jórvík, named by the Danish Vikings who conquered it in 866 A.D. Good thing the name changed, or New Jórvik and New Jersey would both be referred to as N.J.

Why do **we say Magellan was the first to circle the world?**

Portuguese explorer Ferdinand Magellan was the first to find a sea route from the Atlantic Ocean to the Pacific. In 1519, he set out on the first voyage around the world. Before his historic trip, many people believed the world was flat. Magellan left with five ships, but just one made it. Most of the men on the expedition died, including Magellan, who was killed in the Philippine Islands. The survivors were the first Europeans to cross the world's biggest ocean. He named it Pacific for its peaceful, calm waters.

What are **caravels?**

Caravels were the short, speedy ships of choice during the age of sea exploration. They were uncomfortably cramped—rarely longer than 60 feet (18 m)—with sailors packed inside for weeks or months. However, the ships' shallow bottom let them explore narrow coasts and rivers that larger ships couldn't. They were also faster than larger ships, and easier to build. Remember Columbus's *Niña, Pinta,* and *Santa Maria*? The first two were caravels.

Why did a legendary explorer hide in a barrel with his dog?

In 1513, Vasco Nuñez de Balboa became the first European to see the Pacific Ocean from the Americas. With the help of Native American guides, the Spanish conqueror spotted the water from the top of a mountain. He later crossed what is now Panama several more times. But years before he became famous, he was a treasure hunter. And not a very good one. At one point, Balboa and his dog, Leoncico, were broke and stranded on the Caribbean island of Hispaniola. If the two hadn't crawled into a barrel and stowed away on a ship, Balboa would never have gone on to greatness.

Why did did Henry Hudson call himself a failure?

Hudson, an English explorer, was hired by the Dutch in 1609 to find the Northwest Passage, a waterway from Britain to China they thought ran through Canada. The route doesn't actually exist, as he learned while aboard his ship, *Half Moon*. But he did find Manhattan, New York Harbor, the Hudson River, and Canada's huge Hudson Bay. These amazing discoveries didn't stop his men from mutiny—in 1611, his crew forced Hudson, his son, and some sick passengers onto a small lifeboat and set it adrift in the bay. Hudson was never heard from again.

WORLD CULTURE

Why do **Mexicans celebrate the Day of the Dead?** Page 160

Why did **some** countries have colonies?

Colonies are lands and people under the control of a country that is outside of its geographic boundaries. Until the mid-20th century, many large and powerful nations controlled colonies – and their natural resources – for power, money, and influence. By the end of World War II, however, most colonies sought and won their freedom. The U.S.A. was among history's first colonies to successfully fight for its independence.

Why did **countries** come together to create the United Nations?

Until the U.N. was formed in 1945, no international organization had spanned the entire world. But after the devastation of World War II, world leaders wanted to prevent future wars. Fifty-one countries came together on October 24, 1945, in San Francisco, California, dedicated to stopping wars and developing cooperation between nations to promote peace. Now, the organization has 193 member nations.

COOL!

When South Sudan became a country in 2011, it became the 193rd member of the U.N.

Why do **some countries still have kings and queens?**

Until the late 1700s, nearly every nation was led by royalty. Since then, however, most nations that were run by monarchs have turned to a more democratic system. In Britain, for example, the kings and queens were powerful rulers until the Reform Bill of 1832. Now, the royal family performs mainly ceremonial duties.

Why did **countries in Europe form the European Union?**

The European Union (E.U.) was formed in 1993 as a group of countries with similar political and economic goals. The E.U. is dedicated to continuing the peace that was established after the end of World War II. The countries of the E.U. also agree that their sum is greater than their parts economically: by working together, they have more power and success in world markets.

Why are **both French and English official languages in Canada?**

Many of Canada's early European settlers were from France. Their language and culture took root in the country. Today, nearly one-third of Canadians speak French. Public signs are written in French and English, and many kids study both languages. Most French-Canadians live in the province of Quebec.

Why is **Mandarin Chinese the world's most-spoken language?**

One-fifth of the world's people live in China. Mandarin Chinese is the native language of two-thirds of China's people. You do the math! To communicate and trade with so many people, an increasing number of U.S. students are learning to write and speak Mandarin.

COOL!

Japanese has three different alphabets. Kanji uses Chinese characters. Hiragana is used for Japanese words. Katakana is used for words borrowed from other languages. Most Japanese writing combines all three alphabets.

Why did Turkey change alphabets in 1928?

In 1923, when Turkey separated from the Ottoman Empire to become an independent nation, Turkish was written using a version of Arabic letters. To modernize Turkey, the founder of the Turkish Republic, Kemal Ataturk (right), decreed that Turkish would be written using an alphabet of 29 Latin letters, like the letters in our alphabet, along with a few special characters (below).

Ç Ğ Ö Ş Ü

Why is Spanish the official language of so many countries?

Spain controlled colonies in many parts of the world, from South America to the Philippines. Though those countries are now independent, they kept the Spanish language brought by their former rulers. Spanish is the official or primary language in 21 countries, which have about 420 million people. What's more, 10 percent of Americans — another 30 million — speak Spanish.

Why were **shells and salt once considered currency?**

Money only works if everyone agrees to its value. When people first began trading, they needed currency that could represent the same value everywhere. Salt and shells were known by many cultures and came to represent value that everyone could understand. Tobacco, cattle, and even seeds have also been used as currency.

What is a **Canadian loonie?**

Canada's one-dollar coin features a swimming loon, a type of waterfowl. When the coin first came into circulation in 1987, Canadians quickly dubbed it the loonie. The 11-sided coin replaced Canada's paper dollar bill as a cost-saving measure.

Why do some coins have holes?

There's no "hole" answer. Some coins had holes drilled into them to help people carry them on strings, for safety. The square holes seen in many Chinese coins helped with the process of making them—after the metal cooled, the coins were put on a square rod so that their edges could be filed smooth. Some experts say the square represented the Earth, and the circular coin was the surrounding universe.

Why are there **so many kinds of postage stamps?**

Stamps tell a story. The images on them tend to include someone or something important, the amount of money the stamp is worth, and the nation it came from. Stamps vary to make clear the value of the stamp, how it can be used, and where. Also, since stamps are popular to collect, nations are constantly creating new designs to sell.

CRAZY!

The most valuable stamp in the world is a yellow, three-skilling 1855 stamp from Sweden. The one-of-a-kind stamp was sold in 2010 for more than $2.3 million!

Why does **a penny cost more than a penny to make?**

One-cent coins are the most widely circulated unit of money in the U.S. But the value of the penny has been dropping for years. In 2006, it began to cost more than a penny to make a penny. It now costs about 2¢ to make a 1¢ coin. The prices of copper and nickel have gone up, as have the costs of production, creating the unusual situation. Is it time for change?

Why are **steering wheels on the right side of British cars?**

That tradition started centuries ago when British horse riders and cart drivers kept to the left so they could draw their swords with their right hand in the event of an attack. The practice continued with cars—though thankfully, without the swords.

Why do **many countries have a siesta?**

The tradition began in Spain, where it can be very hot in the middle of the day. Workers found that taking a break and a nap in the hot early afternoon enabled them to work longer later. Now, Spain and some other countries still informally observe a midday siesta period for about two hours.

Why is the **number four considered unlucky in China?**

In Chinese, the word "four" sounds like the word for death. There is a similar superstition in Korea, Japan, and Vietnam. Many Chinese people even avoid 14, 24, or any number with a four in it. Many buildings in China do not have floors labeled with that unlucky number.

Why are cows sacred in some cultures?

In many parts of India, cows roam free. Hinduism is the major religion in India. Hindus believe that cows are sacred and are associated with the mother of the gods, so the animals should not be harmed. Believers will drink cows' milk, but will not eat cow meat. As a result, some cows that live in Hindu countries have the freedom to wander wherever they want. Traffic jam!

COOL!

When people give one another flowers in Bulgaria, they make sure that the bouquet always has an odd number of flowers. Even numbers are for funerals.

Why do Scottish men sometimes wear kilts?

A kilt is a sort of wrap that looks similar to a skirt. The men of the Scottish Highlands have worn kilts in several forms since the 1500s. They were such a symbol of Scottish culture – and national pride – that in the 1700s, Great Britain banned all but the military from wearing them for 40 years. They are now frequently worn for formal occasions by Scottish people around the world.

Why do Mexicans celebrate the Day of the Dead?

Día de los Muertos, or Day of the Dead, is celebrated each year on November 1 and 2. Mexicans gather to honor their loved ones who have passed away. People may build altars, visit cemeteries, or offer gifts to the dead. Sometimes, such celebrations can last all night long. *Pan de muerto*, a sweet roll covered in sugar, or *calaveras de azúcar*, sweet treats shaped like skulls, are commonly served.

OUTRAGEOUS!

The United States has a Mother's Day and a Father's Day . . . but no Children's Day! Don't forget to ask WHY!

Why do people leave fruit at Buddhist shrines?

Buddhists often honor their teacher, Buddha, by making an offering at temples or small shrines. The offering, which is usually fruit or other food, encourages sharing, and represents the best part of yourself that you offer to seek blessings from the Buddha.

Why do **the Japanese celebrate Children's Day?**

In Japan, May 5 is Kodomo no hi, or Children's Day. Until 1948, the holiday was intended for boys only, while girls had their own holiday, called Hinamatsuri, or Doll's Day. Now, both girls and boys celebrate with a national festival. Families raise colorful carp flags and fly carp kites. The carp is a fish that swims upstream. It represents strength and determination.

Why is **Ramadan celebrated at a different time each year?**

The Muslim holy month of Ramadan is a time of prayer, fasting, and being with family. The annual celebration, held during the ninth month of the Islamic calendar, begins when a person sees the crescent of the new moon that starts that month. Dates on the Islamic calendar don't line up with the familiar Western calendar, so Ramadan is celebrated during different seasons from year to year.

ARTS & MEDIA

Why are **TV ratings so important?** Page 167

Why are **so many movie studios near Los Angeles, California?**

The first movie cameras needed a lot of light to record images. Indoor lights in the early 1900s were not powerful enough. Los Angeles has sunny weather year-round. The first studio opened there in 1907. As more people in the film industry moved there, more studios opened. Now it's the film capital of the world.

Why are **movie stars paid so much?**

Big stars draw big crowds. Since big box office sales make so much money, big stars can ask for a bigger share of the profits. A hit movie can earn more than $150 million. Without a star to attract an audience, it might earn far less. The stars get paid for helping make the movie a hit.

THE BEATLES

Why are there stars on the sidewalk in Hollywood?

Some cities give their heroes statues. In the Hollywood section of Los Angeles, California, famous entertainers are given metal-and-stone stars on the sidewalks. There are about 2,500 stars on the "Hollywood Walk of Fame." Each star lists the entertainer's name and the way he or she became famous, such as through movies, TV, radio, music, or theater.

Why are the Academy Awards called the Oscars?

Officially, the Academy of Motion Picture Arts and Sciences calls their annual award the "Academy Award of Merit." But the gold statues have been known as Oscars since 1934. One story says that an Academy librarian thought the statue looked like her Uncle Oscar. Another story credits newspaperman Sidney Skolsky with making up the nickname.

CRAZY !

3-D movies aren't new. The first short 3-D films were shown in 1915. The first long features to use the technology were released in 1936 and 1952.

Why does HDTV look different than "regular" TV?

Television stations send picture and sound signals to your home as a stream of constantly changing radio waves. These signals turn hundreds of lines of color into the moving pictures you see on the screen. High-definition TVs (HDTV) receive electronic signals that divide the picture into as many as 1,080 lines —many more than on regular sets. The digital signals deliver crystal-clear images, but better viewing quality can't turn a bad TV show into a good one!

Why are TV stations either broadcast or cable?

Some TV stations send out signals that can be picked up through the air by antennas. The signals are sent out, or cast, over a broad area, coining the name broadcast. But most stations only send their signals directly through cables that run into your home. The TV stations that require you to connect via cable are called—you guessed it—cable.

Why are **TV ratings** so important?

Ratings companies such as A.C. Nielsen and Arbitron measure how many people watch a TV program. The answers help determine the price for the sale of the commercials that run during the program. The TV shows that are most popular are rated the highest. Since companies want their ads to be seen by many viewers, shows with low ratings are often cancelled.

COOL!

Of the ten most-watched TV shows of all time, only two weren't Super Bowls. Both were the final episodes of long-running comedies: M*A*S*H in 1983, and Cheers in 1993.

Why is NFL football so popular on TV?

Over the past few years, NFL games have been among the highest-rated television programs. With so many different programming choices, it's harder than ever to get tens of millions of people to watch the same thing on TV at the same time. But live NFL games often attract huge audiences, because people want to see their team in real time, not watch a recording after the game is over.

Why did **the U.S. government invest in developing the Internet?**

In the late 1960s, the United States Department of Defense helped pay for most of the technology that formed the Internet. The first computers to test the technology were used at universities that were working on behalf of the government, looking for a safe way to communicate with each other. This network grew to become what we know as the Internet and, later, the World Wide Web.

CRAZY!

The World Wide Web was invented by one person! In 1990, Swiss engineer Tim Berners-Lee created the system, which gives a unique address to every spot on the Internet. Web surfing was born!

Why are **hackers so dangerous?**

Billions of people depend on computers and the Internet for access to companies, banks, people, and government services. Hackers are criminal computer whizzes who know how to break into other people's computers, and can destroy those connections and steal data, leaving people without money, privacy, or the ability to do business.

How are modems and routers different?

A modem translates the Internet signal, which usually comes through a cable, so that it can be used by your computer or other device. A router lets a number of devices connect to the modem. Many routers also send a Wi-Fi signal through the air so that you can connect wirelessly. Some modems have a built-in router.

Why do we need browsers to surf the Web?

A Web browser is the software that lets you explore the Internet. A browser reads the codes that are used to name Web pages and other material. It sucks up that information and then funnels it into your computer. Internet Explorer, Safari, Chrome, and Firefox are

Why is William Shakespeare's work called the First Folio?

When William Shakespeare wrote his plays, he did not publish them. Most copies of his scripts were handwritten. When Shakespeare died in 1616, a group of his actors decided to gather 36 of his plays into one collection, which was first published in 1623. The book was a large folio, a format with unusually tall and wide pages. Only about 250 original copies of the First Folio still exist today.

Why are some books hardcover and others paperback?

The first time many books are printed they are sold with hard covers, made of paper and cardboard. These elegant books last longer, but are more expensive. After a while, publishers release the book with a less-expensive paper cover, hoping to sell it to a wider audience. In recent years, this system has been changing —now many books begin as paperbacks and are never printed with hard covers.

COOL!

More than 700,000 new books were published in 2012, the most ever on record for one year. Thanks to Internet tools that let people self-publish their stories and novels, more people can now be authors than ever before.

Why are graphic novels called sequential art?

What do comic strips, comic books, and graphic novels have in common? They tell their stories visually, and the art needs to be shown in a particular order, or sequence. If the art and text were out of order, the story would make no sense. But when told properly, the story unfolds in a wonderful, absorbing way. Silly or serious, any art that depends on showing images in a sequence is called "sequential art."

Why can't most e-books be shared?

When you share a printed book, only one person can keep it. But electronic books, or e-books, are different: one person could buy it and email copies to friends. This may sound like a good deal, but it isn't fair to the publisher and author, who don't get paid for their work. Publishers have developed technology that stops readers from sharing their books to protect their authors and industry.

171

How can one musician play many instruments on the same recording?

The musician isn't playing everything at once. Instead, each instrument is recorded one at a time. Then each of those "tracks" is blended together using computer software to create the entire song.

CRAZY!

The technology used in Auto-Tune was first developed to search for oil underground. Auto-Tune as we now know it was invented in late 1996.

Why do singers use Auto-Tune?

Nobody is perfect, but singers who use Auto-Tune can come close. Auto-Tune software adjusts a vocal recording to the proper note or perfect pitch. Auto-Tune doesn't make it possible for everyone to sing like a pro, but experts believe that many major artists now use this aid to some degree.

Why are some albums called gold records?

If a song or album sells 500,000 copies, the performer is awarded a Gold Record by the Recording Industry Association of America (RIAA). If an album sells a million copies, the performer gets a Platinum Record. The rare album that sells 10 million copies earns a Diamond Record. These awards still look like old-fashioned vinyl record albums.

Why do music recordings need producers?

A producer is part editor, part teacher, and part manager. Producers help musicians plan how to record a song, and make choices for the music. They listen while it's being recorded and help "mix" the recording until it has the sound everyone wants.

Vincent Van Gogh: *Irises*

Why are **Impressionist painters so important?**

For thousands of years, the goal of most artists was to make their pictures look as realistic as possible. But in the late 1800s, a group of artists invented a new approach. They painted their impressions of scenes, rather than exact pictures of what they saw. Impressionism focuses on subtle changes in color brought about by light. At the time, the work of French Impressionist painters like Claude Monet, Edgar Degas, and Pierre-Auguste Renoir was rejected, but now it ranks among the world's most valuable art.

OUTRAGEOUS!

In 2012, a painting by Impressionist artist Paul Cezanne called "The Card Players" sold at auction for more than $250 million. That is currently the highest price ever paid for a work of art. Before that, the record holder was Jackson Pollack's "No. 5 1948," bought in 2006 for $140 million.

Why are some artists folk artists?

A folk artist is usually self-taught , and not trained in any formal way. Folk art usually reflects the traditional culture of the artists, celebrating their community and heritage. This style of art has been around for a long time—the American Folk Art Museum in New York City displays art and objects that date as far back as the eighteenth century.

Why are mobiles known as "kinetic sculpture"?

When something is described as kinetic, that means it involves motion. The mobile is a balanced form of art created from objects dangling from metal rods or wires. A vibration or breeze can make the parts move. The mobile is a relatively new art form, invented in the early 1930s by the American artist, Alexander Calder.

Why is some art called modern even though it isn't new?

The term modern art usually refers to art made between the 1860s and the 1970s. Modern artists rejected many old-fashioned, formal traditions, and expanded beyond paintings to include architecture, dance, and poetry in their movement.

Mark Rothko: from the Seagrams mural series

SPORTS

Why are **Olympic** distances measured in meters?

Page 178

Why are **Olympic distances measured in meters?**

The United States is one of only a few countries that does not use the metric system for measurements. That's why Olympic events involving distances are measured in the units used by most countries: meters and kilometers. Events involving weights use kilograms. Miles, yards, feet, and pounds stay home.

Why does **the winner of the decathlon get the title "the world's greatest athlete?"**

The decathlon is a series of 10 track-and-field events that are held over the course of two days. The events test every part of an athlete's skill: speed, strength, endurance, and the ability to jump and throw. Women compete in the seven-event heptathlon. The better the athlete performs at each event, the more points he or she earns. At the end of the two days, the athlete with the most points wins a gold medal. In 1912, King Gustav V of Sweden called that year's winner, America's Jim Thorpe, "the greatest athlete in the world." The king's words have been repeated ever since.

Why are
the Olympics called
the "modern" Games?

Today's Olympics were inspired by athletic contests first held in Olympia, Greece, almost 3,000 years ago. Athletes from rival cities set aside their differences to pay tribute to the gods. The last ancient Games were held in about 400 A.D. A Frenchman named Pierre de Coubertin revived the tradition in 1896 by organizing a new, modern international competition in Athens, Greece. These events became known as the modern Games.

OUTRAGEOUS!

Baseball and softball were cut from the Olympics in 2008. Before that, polo, tug-of-war, tandem cycling, and rope climbing were taken out, too.

Why is **third base called "the hot corner"?**

No infielder plays closer to home plate than the third baseman. Batted balls come at this player with frightening speed. Hard line drives, sharp grounders, and more—the action gets pretty hot indeed!

COOL! Baseball rules used to be a little different. Until 1884, the pitcher could not throw overhand. He had to pitch sidearm or underhand!

GONZALEZ
33

Price 50 Cents

BATTING and PITCHING,
ILLUSTRATED.

Published by WRIGHT & DITSON,
580 Washington St., Boston, Mass.

Why do **baseball managers wear uniforms?**

Football coaches don't wear pads and most basketball coaches wear business suits. But baseball coaches and managers have to wear the same uniform as their players. The main reason is that in early baseball, managers were also players at the same time. Since they dressed that way then . . . they dress that way now!

Why do **baseball players love donuts?**

They might love to eat them, but that's not what donuts mean in baseball. Hitters put a weighted circle called a donut on their bats and swing them to warm up. The weight loosens their muscles and gets them ready to hit.

Why is a **catcher's gear called "the tools of ignorance"?**

Playing catcher is one of the toughest jobs in sports. You crouch down and stand up hundreds of times per game. Other players run into you. Foul balls and bats bounce off of you. Wearing pads helps, but to most people, it's a position to avoid. In 1939, a catcher named Muddy Ruel nicknamed his gear the "tools of ignorance." He meant that if he had known how much it would hurt, he might have tried pitching instead!

Why was **Jackie Robinson a pioneer?**

Robinson played first base for the Brooklyn Dodgers on April 15, 1947. No big deal, right? Actually, it was far from just another game. Robinson was the first African-American in the Major Leagues in the 20th century. When he broke the "color line," it was considered an American civil rights landmark.

Why do footballs have laces?

There is only one long lace on a football, and it measures about four feet (1.2 meters) long. A football is made of four panels of leather which, though often called pigskin, are made of cowhide. An inflatable rubber bag is placed inside, and a heavy white synthetic cord is laced through holes in the leather to seal it all up. Finally, the rubber bag is inflated until the ball is the correct size for play.

Why are linebackers called Sam, Will, and Mike?

In a three-linebacker formation, the three linebackers play on the strong and weak sides and in the middle. The strong side is the side where the offense's tight end is playing, and the weak side is the opposite. To make calling plays easier, coaches use shorter names for the positions. Sam = strong side; Will = weak side; Mike = middle.

Why is Vince Lombardi famous?

Coach Vince Lombardi's Green Bay Packers won five NFL titles in the 1960s, including the first two Super Bowls. This landed him in the Pro Football Hall of Fame. Lombardi also had a powerful personality and strong opinions that often made news. After he died in 1971, the Super Bowl championship trophy was named in his honor.

Why is a football field painted with hash marks?

Hash marks are the short white stripes on the field. They measure every increment of one yard (0.9 meters) between the 10-yard lines. At the end of each play, the ball is placed on the nearest hash mark. In the early days of football, fields weren't marked. A 1932 snowstorm forced an NFL championship game to be played indoors on a marked field. It worked so well, every field had hash marks the next year.

COOL!

Since 1994, National Football League quarterbacks have had radios in their helmets. Coaches can communicate plays over the helmet's speaker. In 2008, the league also allowed a radio for one defensive player—usually a team captain or a key linebacker.

How are football, soccer, and rugby related?

All three sports grew out of unorganized ball games in England in the 1860s. A meeting in 1863 split rugby and soccer into two sports. (Soccer is called football in most countries outside the United States.) In the U.S., rugby players added changes to the game over time, and it grew into "American" football.

Why was **Earvin Johnson** called "Magic"?

Magic Johnson got his name thanks to his amazing passing ability and his style on the court. A sports writer decided that "Magic" best described the way Earvin played. Until he came along, players of his size (6-foot-9, 220 pounds) rarely played point guard or passed very often. Magic Johnson brought flair to the NBA, where he played from 1979 to 1991, and again during the 1995–96 season.

CRAZY!

The "slam dunk" is a shot in which a basketball player scores by pushing the ball directly through the hoop. It was illegal in college hoops from 1967 to 1976. Other names for the shot include stuff, jam, spike, and throw down.

Why is one play called "pick-and-roll"?

In basketball, a "pick" is a legal block by an offensive player against a defensive player. In the pick-and-roll, a player sets a pick so a teammate can dribble past. The pick-setter then moves, or "rolls," to the basket for a pass—and a shot!

Why was **the three-point shot added to basketball?**

More scoring makes for exciting games. The National Basketball Association added three-pointers in 1979. At the time, ratings for televised basketball games were down because fans were losing interest in the game. In the NBA, a three-point shot must be scored from a distance of at least 23 feet 9 inches (7.24 m) from the hoop.

Why do **basketball players only have five seconds to pass a ball in-bounds?**

Because a Canadian minister and gym teacher named James Naismith said so! He invented basketball in January of 1891 as an indoor activity for students during the coldest months of winter. He wrote down 13 rules for his new game. Part of Rule 9 said that when the ball goes out of bounds, "the thrower-in is allowed five seconds." His original game had 18 players and two peach baskets as goals. Most of his rules are still in place today.

Why do **goalies protect the "five-hole"?**

There are five ways a goalie can miss the puck or ball: above each shoulder, past each leg, or between the feet or knees—that's called the five-hole. The term is used most often in hockey but it can also apply to soccer.

Why is it **called a "hat trick" to score three goals in hockey?**

According to the Hockey Hall of Fame, a Canadian businessman advertised his hats in the 1930s by giving one to any player who scored three goals during a single National Hockey League game in Toronto. Today, hockey fans toss their own caps to the ice in celebration after a player scores three goals. Hundreds of hats are scattered across the rink at some games.

Why is **the hockey championship trophy called the Stanley Cup?**

The cup is named for Lord Frederick Arthur Stanley, the Governor General of Canada. In 1893, he awarded a $50 silver trophy to the Montreal Amateur Athletic Association, the best team in his country. Now each year the cup is won by the top team in the NHL. The original cup was used through 1969, and is in the Hockey Hall of Fame in Toronto, Canada. The modern Stanley Cup has had many sections added to it since its debut in 1970, making it a whole lot bigger… and more valuable.

Why is lacrosse a truly American sport?

Native Americans in the Northeast and Canada played a rough-and-tumble village-vs.-village game, often called *baggataway*. They used woven baskets on sticks to throw and catch a ball. French settlers adopted the game, adapted it, and named it "la crosse" because the sticks looked like the staffs carried by French bishops.

COOL!

The Iroquois Nationals lacrosse team has represented their nation in many international events since 1983, including the World Championships. Its players are often stars on American and Canadian college teams.

5 CANADA

LA CROSSE

POSTES POSTAGE

Why are soccer sidelines also called touchlines?

You might hear British announcers use that word. In Britain, a ball that goes out of bounds is called "into touch," meaning that players may touch the ball to pick it up for a throw-in. For this reason, the lines on the sides of the field that separate touch from "no-touch" are called touchlines. Many other countries use a version of this phrase, too.

How did the game Marco Polo get its name?

The popular pool game of tag is named for Italian explorer Marco Polo, who visited China and other parts of the Far East in the 1200s. There's a story that he got lost in the desert in China and only found his fellow travelers by yelling his own name. In the modern water game, someone plays Marco—keeping his or her eyes closed while counting to 10. Everyone else in the pool scatters quietly. When Marco finishes counting, he shouts, "Marco!" and everyone else responds by yelling "Polo!" Then, Marco swims around the pool, eyes closed, trying to tag someone. If Marco touches you, you're the new Marco.

Why is a badminton birdie also called a shuttlecock?

When the game began in India more than 1,000 years ago, it was called battledore & shuttlecock—early names for the racquet and birdie. In 1873, the Duke of Beaufort played a modern version of the ancient game at his country home in the United Kingdom. Legend says guests at his home stuck goose quills in champagne corks and batted them across the table for sport. The name of the Duke's country home? Badminton.

Why is the little ball in bocce called a pallino?

People have been playing bocce since the days of ancient Rome. This Italian game naturally uses Italian words. *Pallino* means "spot" in Italian, and in the lawn game, that small ball marks the spot, or target. To win, you have to roll your ball closest to the target ball, ideally knocking your opponent's ball out of the way in the process. One large ball is *bocce*, while two or more are *bocci*.

OUTRAGEOUS!

Why are rented bowling shoes often ugly? Mainly so that you won't want to keep them! Shoes bought by frequent bowlers look much more stylish.

Why is table tennis called Ping-Pong?

Table tennis has always been the game's name since it was developed in the late 1800s. John Jacques of Britain coined the name Ping-Pong in 1901 for his brand of table tennis gear. He also introduced the celluloid balls that are used today. The name came from the sound the balls make during play.

INDEX

PHOTO CREDITS

(t: top; b: bottom; r: right; l: left; c: center; bkgd: background)

aKlockwerk: 98t

AP Images: 43b, 45br, 98b, 101c, 106c, 115t, 116, 164t, 164b, 167b, 167b, 175b, 178t, 178b, 179t, 180t, 182b, 183c, 184l, 185r, 186c, 186b

Cal Poly San Luis Obispo: 114r

Sylvain Despretz: 173t

Dreamstime.com: Phil Date 12b; Piotr Marcinski 12t; Berna Namoglu 13tl; 3ddock 15tl; Lisa Young 17br; Dean Bertoncelj 19tl; Zurijeta 20b; Sergiyn 21b; Alexsvirid; Chrispethick 27b; Cammeraydave 28t; Rsazonov 28c; Vladvitek 29br; Youthrstock 32b; Agusesmoris 34t; Katrinaelena 35bl; Eric Hinson 40t; Rozeen Leard 40b; Udra 41tl; Olivier Le Queinec 42b; Evgeny Dubinchuk 43t; Peter Zijlstra 45t; Jeanne McRight 45c; Wayne Stadler 47t; Taiga 47bl; Berislav Kovacević 47r; Lim Seng Kui 48r; Mikhail Dudarev 48b; Mike Kiev 52t; Jippu 2498 54b; Adam Gryko 55t; Qiming Yao 55b; Howard Sandler 56b; Orianna 57t; Ken Backer 57b; R. Gio Santa Maria 76, 85b; Eyewave 78bl; Petro Perutskyy 78cr; Design 56 78cr; Dutchscenery 79t; Rebecca Abell 80b; Tsrphotography 81t; Photoawa 82; Preussureua 83t; Robert Kohlhuber 84t; Empire331 86t; Valya82 87br; Vichaya Kiatying-anguslee 88; Monkey Business Images 91b; Patrick Poendl 92l; Hugo Maes 92; Erik Reis 93b; Edward J. Bock 94bl; Samuel Micut 94r; Eugene Bochkarev 95t; Tonympix 99t; Ladrias81 102; Elena Koulik 104t; Nico Smit 104b; Ivan Cholkov 105t; Brian Kushner 105b; Burly 106t; James Steidl 106b; Olga Besnard 107t; Franco Ricci 107b; MaxiSports 108t; Vvksam 108b; Enrique Gomez 109b; Natalia Shvets 110b; Corepics VOF 111r; Eric Gevaert 111b; Viorel Dudau 113t; Netdoggy 114t; Explorer Media Pty Ltd the Library 115b; Jose Gil 119r; American Spirit 123t; Mikefoto 127c; Emmeci74 127b; Theresa Martinez 128c; John Carter 134; Mikhail Dudarev 134br; Oleksandr Kalyna 134bkgd; Feije Riemersma 138b; Jeniphoto406 140b; Danuer 141t; Robwilson 39 141b; Rafal Cichawa 142b; Dellyne 144b; Hurry 145bl; Alexander Podshivalov 146r; Hans 232 148b; Outline205 150; Carsten Reisinger 152t; Anthony Mcaulay 153b; Rob Van Esch 153t; Fer737ng 154t; Richard Gunion 155b; Windujedi 156t; Peter Spiner 156c; Prostphoto 156b; Mirrormere 158t; Pierre Jean Durieu; Johnnyjoker 160b; Dejan Ljamic 162; Juan Moyano 165b; F9Photos 166t; Ksena2009 166b; Stuart Miles 167br; Pojoslaw 171b; Nikhil Gangavane 172t; Andreykuzmin 173t; Alejandro Duran 175t; Dennis Dolkens 175c; Pneisen 176; Todd Taulman 182t; Lmphot 183t; Raycan 188t; Norman Chan 189c; Ccharleson 189b.

Getty Images: Back cover, bottom: Image Source; Flickr: 9, 11t, 11cl, 13tr, 19tr, 25t, 24b, 24t, 27t, 33br, 34t, 35t, 37b, 44b, 49t, 144t; Cultura 10t; Dorling Kindersley 11tr, 48l, 127t, 137bl; Science Photo Library 13b, 95b; Photographer's Choice 14t, 15b, 33t, 36, 41tr, 83b, 149t, 164t; Taxi 14b, 19b, 86b; E+ 16t, 23, 75b, 93r, 96t, 100br, 110t; Stockbyte 16b, 30br; Image Bank 18t, 21tr, 25b, 29t, 58t, 67br 99b; Peter Arnold 20t; Science Photo Library 21tl; National Geographic 24c; Visuals Unlimited 25c; Minden Pictures 28b; Oxford Scientific 29bl, 32c, 46b; Image Source 32b, 41b, 100t; The Agency Collection 33bl; Stone 36b, 54t; Age Fotostock 37br; Photodisc 39, 159b; Photo Researchers 42t, 58c, 59b, 87bl, 126b; Stockfood Creative 44t; Riser 46l; Aurora+ 50; AFP 49b; OJO Images 52b; Digital Vision 56t; Photononstop 90b; Universal Images Group 58b, 97t, 146t, 155t, 174t; Amana Images 61t; Getty Images News 96b; Eugen Dobric 100t; Getty Images 112t, 124, 125, 131b; SuperStock 118b; Jose Gil 119r; Bridgeman Art Library 121t, 122t, 123b, 138t, 147t; Lonely Planet Images 121b, 160t; Time & Life Pictures 128t, 128b, 165b; Hulton Archive 129t, 181br; Time-Life Images/W. Eugene Smith 129b; Time & Life Pictures/Francis Miller 132t; Time & Life Pictures/Don Cravens: 132b; Archive Photos 133t; Time & Life Pictures/John Bryson 133b; Gallo Images 138c; De Agostini Photo Library 139t, 140t, 148t, 149b; Blend Images 143t; Robert Harding World Images 145br; Tao Images 154b; Brand X Pictures 166t (pilot); Vetta 172t; Getty Images Sport 180b, 187r; Rubber Ball/Erik Isakson 181bl; NBA/Nathaniel Butler 185b; Riser 186t; Datacraft Co. Ltd. 188b; Photodisc 189t.

iStockphoto.com: 10b, 90t

Loke Kun Tan/Starryscapes: 70

NASA Images: 63, 72t, 72b, 73, 101t, 101b, 130l; ESA/NASA/SOHO 64c; JPL-Caltech 66t; JPL/Space Science 67t; JPL 67bl, 97t; Hubble Heritage Team/ESA 68t; Tod Strohmayer (GSFC)/Dana Berry 69t; JPL-Caltech-UMD 71b; Dryden/Jim Ross 104c;

NIWA Science/Miriam Godfrey: 61b

North Wind Picture Archives: 142t

Photos.com: back cover top; 11b, 15tr, 17bl, 26t, 30t, 30bl, 31t, 31r, 31b, 44c, 60c, 60bkgd, 65t, 65b, 66b, 69b, 74t, 74b, 78t, 79b, 81tc, 81c, 81br, 81bl, 84b, 85t, 87t, 93l, 94tl, 113b, 118t, 119l, 120, 157t, 157b, 158c, 161t, 168t, 168b, 169t, 169b, 173b, 179b, 184c, 187l

Rucker Archives: 183b

Basil D. Soufi: 152b

Thomas Schooch: 109t

Shutterstock: Natursports 114b; Sillia Photo 147bl; Elena Terletska 134-35 (5)

Hannah Solomon: 17t, 18b

U.S. Navy: 112r; Ed Early 113c